D0407651

Other Books by Ram Charan

Profitable Growth Is Everyone's Business: 10 Tools You Can Use Monday Morning

What the CEO Wants You to Know

Boards at Work

Books coauthored by Ram Charan:

Confronting Reality: Doing What Matters to Get Things Right
(a best-seller with Larry Bossidy)

Execution: The Discipline of Getting Things Done
(a best-seller with Larry Bossidy)

The Leadership Pipeline: How to Build the Leadership-Powered Company
(with James L. Noel and Steve Drotter)

Every Business Is a Growth Business: How Your Company Can Prosper Year after Year (with Noel Tichy)

E-Board Strategies (with Roger Kenny)

Strategic Management: A Casebook in Policy and Planning
(with Charles W. Hofer, Edwin A. Murray Jr., and Robert A. Pitts)

Custom books for in-house use:

Business Acumen

Making Matrix Organizations a Competitive Advantage

Action, Urgency, Excellence

Boards That Deliver

Boards That Deliver

Advancing Corporate
Governance from Compliance
to Competitive Advantage

Ram Charan

 JOSSEY-BASS
A Wiley Imprint
www.josseybass.com

Copyright © 2005 by John Wiley & Sons, Inc. All rights reserved.

Published by Jossey-Bass
A Wiley Imprint
989 Market Street, San Francisco, CA 94103-1741   www.josseybass.com

No part of this publication may be reproduced, stored in a retrieval system, or trans-
mitted in any form or by any means, electronic, mechanical, photocopying, recording,
scanning, or otherwise, except as permitted under Section 107 or 108 of the 1976 United
States Copyright Act, without either the prior written permission of the Publisher, or
authorization through payment of the appropriate per-copy fee to the Copyright
Clearance Center, Inc., 222 Rosewood Drive, Danvers, MA 01923, 978-750-8400,
fax 978-750-4470, or on the web at www.copyright.com. Requests to the Publisher for
permission should be addressed to the Permissions Department, John Wiley & Sons,
Inc., 111 River Street, Hoboken, NJ 07030, 201-748-6011, fax 201-748-6008, e-mail:
permcoordinator@wiley.com.

Jossey-Bass books and products are available through most bookstores. To contact Jossey-
Bass directly call our Customer Care Department within the U.S. at 800-956-7739, outside
the U.S. at 317-572-3986 or fax 317-572-4002.

Jossey-Bass also publishes its books in a variety of electronic formats. Some content that
appears in print may not be available in electronic books.

Library of Congress Cataloging-in-Publication Data

Charan, Ram.
   Boards that deliver : advancing corporate governance from compliance to competitive
advantage / by Ram Charan.—1st ed.
         p. cm.
   Includes bibliographical references and index.
   ISBN 0-7879-7139-1 (alk. paper)
   1. Boards of directors. 2. Corporate governance. I. Title.
   HD2745.C44 2005
   658.4'22—dc22

                                                       2004025829

Printed in the United States of America
FIRST EDITION
HB Printing   10 9 8 7 6 5 4 3 2 1

Contents

Introduction: Advancing the Practice of
Corporate Governance   ix

Part One: Boards in Transition   1

1   The Three Phases of a Board's Evolution   3
2   What Makes a Board Progressive   14

Part Two: The Three Building Blocks of Progressive Boards   27

3   Group Dynamics   29
4   Information Architecture   47
5   Focus on Substantive Issues   61

Part Three: Contributions That Count   73

6   The Right CEO and Succession   75
7   CEO Compensation   94
8   The Right Strategy   113
9   The Leadership Gene Pool   129
10   Monitoring Health, Performance, and Risk   139

Part Four: Maintaining Momentum   149

11   Board Operations   151
12   Working with Investors   167

Conclusion: Leveraging the Board for
Competitive Advantage   173
Appendix A: Sample Strategy Blueprint   177
Appendix B: The Research Agenda   183

Acknowledgments   187
About the Author   189
Index   191

Introduction:
Advancing the Practice of
Corporate Governance

Make no mistake about it, corporate governance is on the move. New rules and regulations, along with a genuine desire to improve, have caused a perceptible shift in boardrooms across America and around the world. Most CEOs and directors recognize that the journey has just begun, and that they, not regulators, must now lead the way.

This is a book for directors, CEOs, and other business leaders who want corporate governance to be the best it can be. Yes, boards have changed in recent years for the better. But they are not yet fully evolved. Most boards are in flux and still not living up to their potential of providing truly good governance—that is, governance that doesn't just prevent misdeeds but actually improves the corporation. They haven't figured out the "how" of adding value.

That's where this book comes in. It provides the guidance boards need to go from being merely active and in full compliance to making an important contribution to the business. It is a road map for how boards can make the transition to the next step in their evolution, becoming a competitive advantage for their companies. And it is a guidebook for CEOs to see how they can get the most out of their boards.

Beginning with my doctoral work on governance at the Harvard Business School more than thirty years ago, I have closely studied the inner workings of boards. I haven't performed quantitative or statistical correlations between corporate performance and variables of corporate governance. Frankly, such research doesn't get to the causality of what leads to good governance. Rather, I have focused on what happens behind the curtain, so to speak, inside the boardroom. My first book on this subject, *Boards at Work* (published in 1998), described what the best boards were doing at that time.

Since then, through continued research and analysis, I have come to identify three factors that create the foundation for good governance. I have also identified the essential practices and collective behaviors needed to build that foundation—and to build on it. These are practices and behaviors I have observed to have a positive impact on governance for the companies that used them. That is, they seem to be causal factors. They can be adopted by any board to make good governance a reality.

My view of what makes governance good differs from that of so-called board watchers. To them, governance is measured by inputs—the processes and structures used by the board. To the contrary, I believe governance is measured by outputs—the value that a board adds to a corporation. A board's practices are a means by which it can perform good governance, not ends in and of themselves.

Though this book mostly describes practices in the United States, the principles of a board's work hold true around the world. Virtually all nations' corporate codes charge some form of board with the task of ensuring the successful perpetuation of the firm over the long term. The influence of shareholders may be stronger in nations such as the United Kingdom or weaker in nations such as Korea. The composition of boards may emphasize employees in nations like Germany or emphasize independent directors in nations like the United States. Regardless of the differences in mechanics and rules, the board's fundamental mandate is the same—and the characteristics necessary for it to function well are universal.

This book does not describe the myriad requirements for compliance. It doesn't list the rules prescribed by Sarbanes-Oxley, for example, and by the stock market exchanges. CEOs, directors, and general counsels know these rules intimately by now, or have access to comprehensive sources of advice on compliance. The aim here is to prompt boards to continue their momentum, to build on their accomplishments to date, and to put in place the collective behaviors and practices that will allow them to deliver on the promise of good governance once and for all.

The Road Map

Part One of this book identifies the current state of transition many boards find themselves in. Chapter One defines the three evolutionary stages of corporate boards: Ceremonial, Liberated, and Progressive. It ends with a self-test for boards to evaluate themselves—"Where Does Your Board Stand?"

Chapter Two describes the three building blocks that are essential to move from Liberated, where most boards are today, to Progressive. These building blocks are not what external observers are focusing on. Board watchers have become preoccupied with the size of a board, the degree of independence, the number of committees and meetings, the separation of the CEO and Chair positions, and other such variables, none of which gets at the heart of Progressive governance. The true causal factors that lead to better governance are group dynamics, information architecture, and focus on substantive issues, which I outline.

Part Two of the book includes a chapter on each of the three building blocks, to present an in-depth look at the practices and collective behaviors that boards can use to transform themselves into Progressive boards. Chapter Three describes the practices that are essential to the board's group dynamics, the first building block of Progressive boards. Readers will quickly understand how simple techniques can transform the manner in which directors interact with each other, and with management, and become a productive force for governance.

Chapter Four describes the best practices that Progressive boards use to ensure an efficient and productive exchange of information between management and the board. Getting the information architecture right has profound effects on the quality of dialogue in the boardroom.

Chapter 5 describes the best practices that Progressive boards use to focus on substantive issues. Boards' time and attention are very precious. The trap some boards fall into is to allow their time to be dominated by routine financial monitoring and compliance activities. Progressive boards use simple tools to remind themselves of the most critical areas and improve the return on their time.

Part Three of the book includes a chapter on each of five substantive areas where boards can make their most important contributions: the right CEO and succession, CEO compensation, the right strategy, the leadership gene pool, and monitoring health, performance, and risk. In practice, boards tend to give these areas relatively little of their time and attention, yet these are the real opportunities for a board to become a true competitive advantage.

Chapter Six describes tools boards use to ensure they have the leadership they need today and in the future. The right CEO and succession remains job number one for all boards. Every board needs a succession process that draws on the judgments of all directors and leads to high-quality decisions.

Chapter Seven captures an emerging approach to defining CEO compensation, one that provides true alignment between CEO pay and performance. This is an area of critical importance and intense public scrutiny; it behooves all boards to pay close attention to the philosophy behind CEO compensation, as well as to the process of defining the package and the framework that links pay with performance.

Chapter Eight describes how boards can ensure they stand behind the right strategy. There are very specific practices that Progressive boards use with great effectiveness to get a full and shared understanding of strategy—a source of misunderstanding on Liberated boards—as well as to help shape the strategy. Appendix A builds on this chapter to present a sample of a strategy blueprint that can jump-start discussion.

Chapter Nine lays out the approach that Progressive boards use to make sure the company is developing its leaders at all levels. The leadership gene pool is an essential component of the company's ability to create value and sustain a competitive advantage over the long term. And a strong leadership gene pool will make the CEO succession process more robust in the future.

Chapter Ten helps boards go beyond the usual in monitoring health, performance, and risk. Progressive boards dwell relatively little on routine financial figures that describe yesterday's performance; they cut to the core issues of financial health, the factors that drive tomorrow's performance, and the dangerous interactions of risk.

Finally, Part Four provides a pragmatic approach to maintaining momentum. Chapter Eleven contains advice on a range of less important factors under the rubric of board operations, including the logistics of board meetings. Chapter Twelve deals with investors, who are increasingly vocal constituencies. But not all investors are alike. Boards should know how to filter the legitimate concerns from the self-serving voices.

Appendix B is addressed to readers interested in pursuing research in this area. I propose an approach that will generate better insights into corporate governance and uncover the real factors that underlie effective governance. Resulting research will provide boards with better guidance on how to improve.

Looking Ahead

The opportunity for boards to add value is very real. What's more, the desire and motivation of directors to realize the opportunity is evident. With the right set of practices, any group of directors can become a board that delivers value to management and to investors.

The board sits in a critical position in the modern free enterprise system. It has the responsibility, as well as the opportunity, to make a significant difference. The chapters that follow are suggestions to all directors so they can fulfill their responsibility and achieve their opportunity.

Boards That Deliver

Part One

Boards in Transition

Around the world, boards have accepted a new mandate and are adopting a new mindset toward their work. But living up to new expectations is posing a challenge for many boards. Understanding the true nature of the transformation corporate governance is undergoing can help directors recognize where they are getting stuck, why, and how to move forward.

Chapter One describes three phases boards go through—from Ceremonial to Liberated to Progressive—as they try to increase their contribution to the corporation. Many boards today are stuck in the middle phase and therefore do not add as much value as they could.

Chapter Two explains what makes a board Progressive, the third phase of board evolution. Three building blocks must be in place for boards to make a substantive contribution to the business.

Chapter One

The Three Phases of a Board's Evolution

Boards of directors have undergone a rapid transformation since the Sarbanes-Oxley Act of 2002. The shift in power between the CEO and the board is perceptible. Directors are taking their responsibilities seriously, speaking up, and taking action. It's a positive trend and an exciting time for boards.

But the evolving relationship between the CEO and the board has yet to find the right equilibrium in most cases. It's important that boards become active, but there is danger in letting the pendulum swing too far. Astute directors and CEOs sense the tension. They recognize that just as past practices have failed them, recent attempts to make the board a true competitive advantage are not always hitting the mark.

Here's one example. In the spring of 2003, a CEO approached me at a conference. "Something's gnawing at me," he said.

"What do you mean?" I asked, with some surprise. "I saw your latest earnings report and it looks like you're really delivering." This was true. I knew the company went through a period of adjustment following the recession, but business had rebounded and the company was turning niche products into real growth opportunities both domestically and abroad. "Is there some bad news that you're not making public?"

"No, no. It's not that, Ram," said the CEO, whom I'll call Jim Doyle. (He, like some of the other executives I spoke with in researching this book, would prefer to remain anonymous.) "The business is rock solid. We're executing well."

"Well, it sounds like you've got it all together," I said.

Then came the punchline: "It's the board."

I let Jim continue. "I took over from Alan three years ago. Before that, I was president and I remember how Alan ran board meetings. There was essentially no dialogue; communication was a one-way street. When I became CEO, I wanted the board to help me. I wanted to make it a modern board. So we made all the structural changes that have been asked of us, like changing the composition of the Audit Committee. We now have eleven directors; eight of whom are independent by any definition. Only two directors are holdovers from the old board. We have eight full-day meetings per year, and everyone participates. The boardroom is very lively," Jim explained.

"Sounds like you're doing all the right things," I said.

"I thought so. But lately, I've heard more and more questions in our meetings. Now I don't mind fielding questions from directors. In fact, I consider it their job to ask questions and my job to address those questions. But some of the questions and the analyses directors ask for are off the wall. I'm getting sidetracked covering all of them. And the same questions keep coming up. It's frustrating and I know some directors are frustrated, too."

"Give me an example, Jim?"

"Sure. I presented our new strategy to the board several times and they tell me in the boardroom that they support it. But after some one-on-one chats, I began to realize that not everyone gets it. So we held a retreat last weekend, and I brought in the brand-name strategy firm that helped design the strategy to present it," Jim said.

"Let me guess, they flipped through a deck of a hundred Power-Point slides," I conjectured.

"I admit that I probably let the consultants show a few too many slides," Jim said. "But within thirty minutes, two directors began to go off on minutiae. Charlie told us he didn't believe the media strategy was appropriate. Then he said he didn't like the national TV ads he saw last week. He thought regional advertising would be more effective than national TV ads. This was during a discussion that was supposed to be dedicated to strategy. The other directors bit their tongues. Later on, Jeff started in on how he thought discounts were too high for large customers. He wouldn't let it go, even though he knew we depend on our ten biggest customers for thirty percent of our revenues. Needless to say, the re-treat fell apart and we accomplished very little. When we adjourned, everyone told me, 'we support you,' but their body language said something different."

"How long has this been going on?" I asked.

"I'd say off and on for the past three meetings. Some directors keep coming back with the same questions over and over. It's very draining. I need to find a way to get us on track."

Jim's five-minute story matched what I've seen happen too often. Since Sarbanes-Oxley, I've heard variations of his story many times. Directors have turned the corner in their attitudes toward directorship and are devoting more time and energy to the job. But they are still searching for ways to make a meaningful contribution to the business.

The Real Risk of Value Destruction

Jim's board, like most boards in the post–Sarbanes-Oxley world of corporate governance, is very different from its counterpart of a dozen years earlier. It's not that the directors themselves are markedly different. By and large, boards still consist of smart, trust-worthy people—individuals with backgrounds of achievement and ability who are a credit to the firms on whose boards they serve. In some cases, in fact, the new directors of a dozen years ago are the very same wise sages on today's boards.

The change in boardrooms today is not marked by the people but rather by the social atmosphere. Boardrooms have more energy, liveliness, inquisitive interactions among directors, and thoughtful engagement by CEOs. The difference today is a mindset, an emerg-ing collective desire to do something meaningful. It appears that boards of directors, as an institution, are coming of age.

Much of the public outcry—and resulting regulation—of re-cent years is based on the failure of boards to root out fraud, some of which destroyed whole companies. But boards are recognizing that they have failed in another, arguably more widespread, way: by allowing (sometimes inadvertently contributing to) faltering performance. Entire industries collapsed in the wake of the dot-com bust; too many companies failed to adapt their businesses to the different external environment after the recession began and after the 9/11 tragedy. No one could have foreseen global terrorism, but what about anticipating the fallout from the go-go years of the New Economy, or not recognizing the importance of emerging new channels? Couldn't boards have prompted their managements to pinpoint and consider these issues?

In some cases, boards have made costly mistakes. How about hiring a CEO from the outside who is a master of cost-cutting—when the company needed a leader who could grow the business? Or tying the CEO's incentives to the wrong goals? Or approving a grand growth strategy with an unhealthy appetite for risk?

Most boards want to do the right thing, whether it's complying with the new rules (and there are a lot of them) or contributing in substantive ways on matters of choosing the CEO, compensating top management, ensuring that the company has the right strategy, and providing continuity of leadership and proper oversight. Their commitment and level of engagement marks a new stage in their evolution.

The good news is that these boards are unlikely to commit the sins of omission that were common among the passive, CEO-dominated boards just a few years ago. The bad news is that they are now vulnerable to committing sins of commission. That's because past board experience has not fully prepared directors and CEOs for the challenges they face today. Without clear guidelines to take them forward, well-meaning boards such as Jim Doyle's can actually erode the vitality of the company and drain time and energy from the CEO. It's a real danger, and companies truly suffer when this happens.

To achieve their full potential, boards must continue to evolve. They must make a conscious effort to go to the next level.

The Evolution of Boards

Boards began their evolution in the pre–Sarbanes-Oxley era of passivity. Back then, they were "Ceremonial" boards, because they existed only to perform their duties perfunctorily. Sarbanes-Oxley has driven many boards to a second evolutionary phase; directors have become active and "Liberated" themselves from CEOs who previously dominated the boardroom. But there is also a third phase awaiting boards, when active directors finally gel as a team and become "Progressive."

The Ceremonial Board

A decade ago, when one non-executive director joined the board of a paragon of American industry, a long-serving colleague told him, in private, "New directors shouldn't speak up during board meetings for the first year." That attitude is untenable today and, in fact, that board is much different now. But such comments are indicative of the culture of passivity that permeated the Dark Ages of corporate governance.

Some readers may remember when such Ceremonial boards were commonplace. Management had all its ducks in a row by the time a board meeting began. There was a scripted morning presentation that was rehearsed to the second in a tight agenda. The CEO communicated very little with the board between meetings, other than with the one or two confidants the CEO trusted and worked with if the need arose.

These boards perfunctorily performed a compliance role. Many directors served for the prestige and rarely spoke among themselves without the CEO present. They made sure to fulfill their explicit obligations, including attending the required board meetings and rubber-stamping resolutions proposed by management. "An important trait of boards during this era," observes Geoff Colvin, senior editor at large at *Fortune* magazine and co-host of the Fortune Boardroom Forum, "is that they were largely anonymous to the public. The general interest media rarely reported directors' names. So back then, the prospect of shame and embarrassment when a company ran into trouble wasn't much of a threat." Such were the norms and expectations of directorship during this era.

Most readers will recall a few boards that fit this description at some point in time. Hopefully, it doesn't sound like any boards on which they now serve, though these boards do still exist.

The Liberated Board

Most boards left their Ceremonial status behind after the passage of Sarbanes-Oxley. A new generation of CEOs now expects boards to contribute. And candidates for directorship now expect active participation as a condition of their acceptance. There is a general sense of excitement as directors embrace an active mindset.

The transition to liberation had really begun about a decade earlier. In 1994, the General Motors board, advised by Ira Millstein, first published its "Guidelines for Corporate Governance." The document was widely praised as a model for corporate boards. *BusinessWeek* even called it a "corporate Magna Carta," referring to the document signed in 1215 by King John that stipulated, among other things, that no one, including the King, is above the law.

The comparison was fitting; GM's CEO and Chair, Robert Stempel, stepped down late in 1992 after losing the confidence of GM's non-executive directors. When the non-executive directors named one of their own as Chair, it signaled a distinct change in the general attitude of boards as passive bodies. No one dreamed such a thing would happen at the world's largest company. Many directors around the country took note. In particular, the boards of several prominent bellwether companies, including those at American Express, AT&T and IBM, followed GM's lead.

Still, not that many boards entered the ranks of the Liberated in the 1990s. Though board watchers and activists such as Bob Monks, Nell Minow, Sarah Teslik, Richard Koppes (of Calpers), and others pressed for reform, many companies under fire were reluctant to make wholesale changes in their governance practices.

There was no urgency for change until the scandals broke at Enron, WorldCom, Tyco, HealthSouth, Adelphia, and elsewhere. Then came the rapidly passed Sarbanes-Oxley Act of 2002, with its broad provisions on Audit Committee work, internal controls, and fraud prevention, along with the ensuing reforms enacted by the Securities and Exchange Commission and the stock exchanges, lawsuits filed against directors and corporate officers, and the public embarrassment of some very experienced directors. With so much shareholder and bondholder value evaporated in the scandals, the capital markets also began paying closer attention to corporate governance and to the possibility of pricing the perceived quality of transparency and governance into securities.

Directors saw their peers chastised and overwhelmingly heard investors' calls to become active. Although some boards remain Ceremonial today, the pendulum swung decidedly toward Liberated boards. In many cases, incoming CEOs helped drive the change.

Liberation is good news. But while liberation can mean a high-functioning team, it can also mean each director singing a different tune. If it's not handled effectively, liberation can inadvertently make CEOs and management less effective, and can adversely affect the creation of shareholder value. It happens. Liberated directors often play to their own strengths individually, not as a collective body. They ask of their CEOs too many things, some of which are plainly minutiae or irrelevant. The limited time that these CEOs have to run their companies gets further diluted. This is the state in which so many Liberated boards sit today—though certainly not by intention.

The Progressive Board

The intent of directors who have liberated themselves is for their boards to become what I call "Progressive." They comply meticulously with the letter of the law, and they also embrace its spirit. Further, they aim, as Andy Grove, founder, former CEO, and current Chair of Intel, is quoted by *Fortune* magazine as saying, "to ensure that the success of a company is longer lasting than any CEO's reign, than any market opportunity, than any product cycle" (August 23, 2004, p. 78).

To achieve this broader mandate, these boards become uniformly effective as a team, and they make their value evident while maintaining an independent viewpoint. Directors on a Progressive board gel into a coherent and effective group. All directors contribute to a dialogue that has lively debates, sticks to key issues while dropping tangents, and leads to consensus and closure. They challenge each other directly, without breaking the harmony of the group and without going through the CEO. Directors find the give-and-take in board meetings energizing. They enjoy the intellectual exchange, and they learn from each other. They look forward to meetings.

The board and the CEO have a working relationship that is constructive and collaborative, but board members are not afraid to confront hard issues. The lead director, or whoever facilitates executive sessions, is a liaison between the board and management who keeps executive sessions focused and running smoothly, and is very effective at communicating the heart of the board's viewpoint, not a collection of opinions from individual directors, to the CEO. Feedback is constructive and highly focused in a way that helps the CEO. CEOs respect the Progressive board's role and contribution, and are collaborative in their approach to the board.

The Progressive board adds value on many levels without becoming a time sink for management. The diverse perspectives of directors on the external environment, including legislative affairs, economic changes, global business, and financial markets, are a boon to management's strategy-setting and decision-making efforts. Directors contribute most where their interest, experience, and expertise are greatest, and they know their viewpoints are expected. Directors also add value through their judgments on and suggestions for the CEO's direct reports.

Progressive boards take their own self-evaluation—of the collective body as well as of individual board members—very seriously. There is a sincere effort to implement the findings of the evaluation on both a board and individual director level.

In short, Progressive boards move the essence of their governance activities to comprise not only complying with changing rules and norms but also adding value to the long-term potential of the company. These boards are a competitive advantage in and of themselves.

Becoming a Progressive board is not beyond reach. Such boards exist at some of the largest companies in America, like General Electric, as well as at mid-caps like MeadWestvaco and smaller public companies, like PSS/World Medical. The completion of this transformation is very much up to the CEO and the board. The first step is to realize where you are today; the diagnostic at the end of this chapter can help a board realize where it stands and in what areas it could improve. Liberated boards like Jim Doyle's don't need dramatic overhauls. But they do need to recognize what is holding them back; the diagnostic can help. After that, it's up to the directors and management to take conscious steps to change. The next three chapters are designed to help boards speed their transition.

Where Does Your Board Stand?

The following questions constitute a diagnostic to help boards figure out where they stand. Answering these questions is not an academic exercise. The goal is to identify how a board could improve and move to the next level. Indeed, the awareness of the need for continuous improvement is one characteristic of a Progressive board.

The numerical scores in the diagnostic don't lead to a "rating" of a board's effectiveness. Rather, the pattern of responses will reveal the areas that a given board might wish to address. Lower scores in any one category—group dynamics, information architecture, or focus on substantive issues—should be a flag that the board needs to focus on those issues.

Group Dynamics

1. Does the board consistently bring dialogue on critical topics to a clear closure, with consensus? Or is dialogue fragmented?

1	2	3	4	5
fragmented				consensus

2. Do all directors freely speak their minds on key points?

1	2	3	4	5
seldom				always

3. Do directors respond to each other during board meetings, particularly when they don't agree with each other? Or do directors engage in dialogue solely addressing the CEO?

1	2	3	4	5
CEO				directors

4. Have board meetings focused on the most important issues, as defined jointly by the board, the committee Chairs, and management? Or have they wandered into minutiae or tangents?

1	2	3	4	5
tangents				focused agenda

5. Does the board feel that the company is getting a return on the time the board is spending on corporate affairs? Or does the board feel their time is not very productive?

1	2	3	4	5
not very productive			good return on time	

6. Do directors individually feel they get something out of board meetings? Or is it a chore and a burden?

1	2	3	4	5
chore			learn something every time	

7. Is the dynamic between the board and the CEO adversarial or constructive?

1	2	3	4	5
adversarial				constructive

8. Have directors acted on feedback that emerged from a real and constructive self-evaluation?

1	2	3	4	5
no individual evaluations			personally made improvements	

Information Architecture

9. Is sufficient time given for discussion in the boardroom? Or are presentations scripted to the second with no time left for dialogue?

1	2	3	4	5
fully scripted			discussion built in	

10. Is information presented in a way that leads to useful insights that facilitate productive discussion?

1	2	3	4	5
no insights			leads to insights	

11. Does the board go out on its own to learn about the company (visiting plants) and the industry?

1	2	3	4	5
not at all			board takes initiative	

12. Does the CEO feel comfortable discussing bad news and uncertainties with the board?

    1   2   3   4   5
    good news only   bad news, too

Focus on Substantive Issues

13. Has the board discussed succession in depth during recent meetings? Or is it waiting until succession nears?

    1   2   3   4   5
    waiting   discussed recently

14. Do all directors fully understand the philosophy underlying their CEO compensation plan?

    1   2   3   4   5
    not discussed   philosophy understood

15. How clear is each director on the strategy going forward?

    1   2   3   4   5
    unclear   clear

16. How well has the board bought into the company's strategy?

    1   2   3   4   5
    not at all   totally

17. Has the board discussed with management the potential risks inherent in its strategy? Or has it left risk management to management?

    1   2   3   4   5
    left to management   full discussion of risk

18. Does the board explicitly monitor financial health and operating performance relative to the competition by focusing on causal factors?

    1   2   3   4   5
    financial measures   causal factors

19. How familiar is the board with the leadership gene pool and efforts to develop up-and-coming managers?

    1   2   3   4   5
    not very familiar   very familiar

Chapter Two

What Makes a Board Progressive

An energized and active board is no guarantee of good governance. Indeed, when a Liberated board fails to fully evolve and gel into a cohesive body, it can be a serious problem for the business.

In one board meeting, for example, a director demanded that a version of the company's strategy be produced with a ten-year time horizon. "What will we be when we grow up?" he asked, just before he expounded on the ten-year master plan for his own company. After an awkward silence, the CEO promised to come up with an analogous ten-year plan. The other directors knew the company was in a turnaround; the industry was changing so rapidly that mapping out actions beyond three or four years was pointless. Hearing the one director's request with no dissenting opinions, the CEO and his team burned valuable time developing this academic exercise.

At another company's board meeting, a director asked detailed questions about productivity and utilization at the plant level. This director, a manufacturing vice president at his own company, felt a need to show off his expertise in this area. But the minutiae evident in his questions was irrelevant to the board.

Even more extreme, though rare, is the situation at a third company, a market share leader for thirty years that lost its way. The CEO saved the company from a hostile takeover and had the company operating respectably. Furthermore, he was successful in activating his board of directors, convincing them to speak up in the boardroom and emerge from Ceremonial status.

Unfortunately, two articulate and outspoken directors hijacked boardroom dialogue. One, a tenured finance professor at one of the top business schools in the nation, hounded the CEO for achieving 8.5 percent return on assets—within the top industry quartile but below his target of 10 percent. The second, a driven executive who had been denied the CEO position at two other companies, continually nitpicked over similar minutiae. The CEO repeatedly told the board that these discussions were narrow, but no other directors rose to his defense.

Eventually, the CEO left the firm in frustration. A successor was promoted internally, and conditions got worse. Return on assets dropped to 5 percent and growth was stagnant for years. Later, the successor took on a huge amount of debt to make an acquisition—and the company went bankrupt as the business cycle changed. The first CEO, incidentally, is doing very well for his new firm.

The bottom line is that Liberated boards have an enormous opportunity to add value to the companies they serve. But they also run the risk of eroding value. For this reason, boards must inject urgency in accelerating their transformations.

The Basic Building Blocks

After CEOs and directors diagnose where they stand in the evolutionary scale, they should be ready to take action on that diagnosis. To do this, they should understand the three building blocks described in this chapter that truly differentiate Progressive boards:

- *Group dynamics:* The tenor of interactions among board members and between the board and management is a fundamental difference between Ceremonial, Liberated, and Progressive boards.
- *Information architecture:* How boards get what information, and in what form, is vital to how the board operates. The mechanisms are typically very different for boards at different stages.
- *Focus on substantive issues:* What boards focus their time and attention on will determine whether boards are able to add value consistently.

Exhibit 2.1 sketches the differences among the phases of board development.

In reality, a wide range of behaviors and effectiveness occur in each phase of board evolution. Each board has distinct characteristics regarding the three building blocks. Some Liberated boards, for example, struggle with their group dynamics and with changes in their relationships with their CEOs. But others have excellent group dynamics, while they struggle to balance their time around the central issues and the full scope of their responsibility. The labels are useful in understanding the dramatic differences between boards of the past, boards of the present, and, hopefully, boards of the future. But directors should realize that there is a continuum within each phase.

With the building blocks in place, a board has the opportunity to make contributions that count. Diligence in five areas, as described briefly in the second part of this chapter, can make boards a competitive advantage.

Progressive boards also need to beware of mechanics. Progressive boards conform to changing rules and norms, but they quickly find a way to move beyond them to address more substantive issues. The problem of mechanics is discussed at the end of this chapter.

Group Dynamics

The first building block of Progressive boards is group dynamics. The effectiveness of a board depends not only on the quality and diverse capabilities of the individuals on the board but also on the quality of their interactions. The phrase "group dynamics" is a catch-all to describe the latter. It's an amalgamation of directors' relationships with one another and with the CEO, and their dialogue and behaviors in the group setting.

On Ceremonial boards, directors were silent; thus, group dynamics was not an issue. But in a Liberated boardroom, directors are active—sometimes too active. Their questions and commentaries tend to be highly fragmented. Directors are unable to gel into a cohesive body and create a unified point of view or message for management. The whole does not become greater than the sum of the parts.

Exhibit 2.1. The Phases of Boards.

	Phase 1: Ceremonial	Phase 2: Liberated	Phase 3: Progressive
Group Dynamics	CEO all powerful; directors passive. No productive dialogue in boardroom.	Directors free to speak up in boardroom *but* . . . dialogue is fragmented, a few directors overstep bounds, tangents drain energy, and most of the time no consensus is reached. Board pledges to improve *but* . . . focuses on mechanical solutions and does not act on self-evaluation with conviction.	Directors gel as a group. Mutual respect and trust among directors and management. One or two directors emerge as facilitators to channel lively debates. Everyone participates and consensus is very frequently achieved on key issues. Self-evaluation gives tool for continuous improvement and directors take results seriously.
Information Architecture	Management tightly controls information flow. Usually not the right amount of information. Information is summarized at very high level, and presentations run long.	Management willingly makes company transparent to board *but* . . . is frustrated by ad hoc demands by some directors that leave management scrambling. Board asks for more information *but* . . . what they get is not packaged well and doesn't help the directors understand the guts of the business.	Information is focused, timely, regular, and digestible. Management anticipates board needs. Directors learn the business.
Focus on Substantive Issues	Compliance only. Usually rubber-stamps CEO's decisions.	Board desires to make a contribution *but* . . . overwhelmed by issues, becomes driven by compliance and routine operating issues.	Board and CEO jointly set twelve-month agenda. Board focuses on issues that are value-added and anticipatory, as well as those that are compliance-related.

What makes it challenging for directors to gel is the fact that boards are unlike most other social bodies in several key respects. First, boards consist of individuals who are assembled without a final arbiter. Most teams have a clearly defined manager, captain, or at least someone who, at the end of the day, makes final decisions and is held accountable for them. When the group hits an impasse, fails to produce, or is held hostage by an uncooperative member, the leader and team members have some recourse. Not so for boards.

Second, boards collectively have great power, but each director has little individual power. Thus the group needs to form a consensus, often without taking votes, and again without a final arbiter. Some directors aren't used to that.

Third, a board is made up of highly respected peers. They are leaders in their respective fields. Individual directors are strong and confident, yet in a group of peers, some hold back lest they risk losing respect. Unless directors learn to proffer dissent productively, this "code of congeniality" can suppress debate as directors avoid contradicting one another directly. This is an adjustment for many.

Progressive boards make their group dynamics work. They do not end a dialogue without making sure all voices have been heard and without coming to an explicit consensus on key matters.

Many times, directors are aware that the group dynamics is failing, that boardroom dialogue is not satisfactory, but they don't know how to change. They may sense that one or two other directors have their own agendas. They may see a director or two repeatedly dragging the dialogue off on tangents, dwelling on insignificant issues, or putting the CEO on the defensive. Whatever the symptoms, in the early stages of Liberation, the board's return on time, as well as the CEO's, is very low. Increasing the length of meetings or holding more meetings will not help.

The relationship between the board and the CEO, particularly the power dynamics between the two, is among the most essential elements of group dynamics. On Ceremonial boards, the problem is the traditional one—the CEO holds all the power. When a board moves from Ceremonial to Liberated, there is flux in the power relationship. The CEO cedes some power and authority to the board as a group, but as this pendulum swings, problems can emerge.

The first problem is that a board can overstep its bounds. Some directors interpret their new mandate as the need to take charge and put down what they now see as the CEO's unchecked power. But behaving in a way that tries to assert authority in the name of independence, as some directors on Liberated boards do, creates an adversarial board-CEO relationship that is counterproductive.

Directors on Progressive boards recognize that they are free to challenge the CEO. As Jeff Immelt, CEO and Chair of General Electric, says, "Everyone understands that [senior management] ultimately works for the board and for the investors." But directors at GE and other Progressive boards do so in a manner that respects management's role. They improve the CEO's effectiveness. The only time the board-CEO relationship becomes adversarial is when a major problem leads to a consensus for the CEO to resign.

The second and more subtle problem occurs when a board is not functioning well as a group and a power vacuum emerges. CEOs may ask their boards for input, but if the directors speak their minds without coalescing around a distinct viewpoint and they expect the CEO to accommodate all of their responses, the CEO's focus gets diluted.

"Everyone wants to be heard," says Lars Nyberg of the new boardroom climate. Nyberg is former CEO and current Chair of NCR, as well as Chair of Micronic Laser Systems AB in Sweden and a director of Snap-On, the automotive tool manufacturer, and Sandvik, the Swedish machine-tool and specialty materials maker. "You run the risk of having a CEO record every director's wishes, ending up with a 50-point list. It's a sure way to kill a company."

The power vacuum can also exist on the other side of the relationship. Some very polite CEOs won't confront what needs to be confronted in the boardroom. Whether it's because of time pressure or a fear of rocking the boat, these CEOs don't engage in the discussion or push back against a director, even when the director seems to be off base. Push back too hard, and the CEO sounds defensive and unwilling to listen to the board. Push back too softly, and the CEO can appear passive or weak. The board's perception of weakness can undermine the CEO's authority. When adverse conditions arise, the weakened relationship can prevent the company from reacting decisively.

A third power problem that can emerge is among the members of the board itself. Cliques naturally form within groups. Long-serving directors often sit together and drop sideways comments or embark on whispered conversations. It can be distracting. In the extreme case, a vocal director can form a coalition and drive issues forward without true board consensus. This has happened more than once.

When boards gel together as a cohesive group, power is not an issue in the board-CEO dynamics. Directors have a shared under-standing of their purpose and mandate. The board and the CEO understand their roles vis-à-vis each other; the board knows how to get consensus on its action items, and how to provide input to the CEO. Progressive boards also know that though directors need to be comfortable challenging the CEO in order to perform mean-ingful oversight, individual directors should not adopt an adver-sarial stance.

Sometimes it's hard for directors to know how they can gel into an effective board. But the mindset of identifying the shortcom-ings and taking steps to improve is built into the self-evaluation process for Progressive boards. For Liberated boards, self-evalua-tion is little more than a box-ticking exercise. Rarely does it draw out the real issues that block the board from making a substantive contribution.

Progressive boards, on the other hand, are careful to include group dynamics in their evaluation and use a process that makes it easy for sensitive issues to surface. Their whole approach to self-evaluation reinforces the idea that each director is expected to con-tribute not only to the substance of deliberations but also to the basic functioning of the group. And they are always prepared to act on the critical findings of the evaluation.

Information Architecture

Most directors would agree that no single director will ever know the business as well as management does. Period. There is simply too much going on in the company and in the industry for any part-time director to keep current.

Thus directors must continuously learn about the company. And they must all have the same foundation of information for their dialogue to be productive. If they cannot get the right information efficiently and in the right form, the best board dynamics in the world won't help the board get its job done.

Most of that information comes from management. The general feeling among Liberated boards, however, is that the reports they get before board meetings don't fit the bill. Directors are uniformly frustrated by the low quality of information they get. Sometimes they get a hundred-page packet filled with jargon and financial minutiae a week before a meeting. Sometimes they have difficulty getting any information at all from management.

Whether the data is too much, too little, or too poorly presented, boards spend a lot of board meeting time questioning management about the meaning of data they have received. "I feel like a prosecuting attorney," one director said of his attempts to get details of a company's operating performance. This leaves directors unprepared for substantive discussion, even if there were plenty of time for it.

There's frustration from management, too. If boards demand more and more granularity, they can become a nuisance to management. Boards have to be conscious of how much work they are piling on their CEOs—and make sure the work they are asking of their CEOs is the right work, as the whole board sees it.

Progressive boards work with management to design in advance what information they need. Directors put their heads together with the CEO not only on what information is provided but also on how and when it is provided. This way, the board knows what to expect and when to expect it. This ensures that the quality, timeliness, content, and format of information facilitates insights and reactions from directors. By understanding the meaning and context of the information, whether about the external environment or internal operations, directors are in a position to discuss the future of the company as the information indicates, rather than discussing the meaning of the information itself.

Getting the information flow right is a tremendous benefit to management. CEOs and CFOs for the most part want to make the business transparent to directors, but they don't want to spend their time explaining financial statements line by line. When the board and management are on the same page to begin with, this problem is greatly reduced.

Progressive boards also spend time and effort outside the boardroom learning about the business. They hear from employees and analysts; they visit stores and manufacturing plants. They find ways to keep their finger on the pulse of the company, which keeps their questions and opinions sharp and on target.

Focus on Substantive Issues

With the right group dynamics and efficient information flow, the board can get down to its real work. It's important, however, that the board sees the big picture in terms of its total responsibility—the substance of its deliberations. Is it allocating enough time for the most important issues? Is it missing anything? Is it anticipating issues and opportunities?

Compliance with the rules of governance is a necessity. What remains to be seen is whether boards will do more. Many boards spend a lot of time discussing the minor issues or getting bogged down in compliance, then feel rushed when it comes to the real opportunity to add value. They cover important topics as they emerge, but wonder if they could be more proactive and anticipatory. Even though they spend many hours outside the boardroom on governance issues, directors have difficulty balancing their time and attention on the breadth of issues in the limited time they have together (some forty-eight to sixty hours a year in face-to-face board meetings).

Progressive boards get compliance to right and also focus on issues that add real value to management and to shareholders. They avoid adding to a laundry list of items. They work together to define the issues that should command the board's attention and are vigilant about managing their time accordingly.

They provide a similar focus for management by distilling the few central thoughts the CEO must consider. "Management is all about priorities," says Nyberg. "The board has to come together and say these are the top five priorities for the coming four quarters." Or the CEO could articulate the most important points and see if the directors agree. Either way, there must be a shared understanding of what is most important and how directors and management will focus their limited time and energy.

Contributions That Count

Building the foundation for the board to be effective must come first. Unless that happens, attempts to make substantive contributions are likely to founder and frustrate directors and the CEO. Getting the group dynamics, information architecture, and focus right allows boards to exercise their common judgments on crucial topics.

With the three building blocks providing a solid foundation, boards can begin to add value. Best practices in five important areas help Progressive boards apply their wisdom and experience to contribute to the long-term health and prosperity of the business:

- The right CEO and succession
- CEO compensation
- The right strategy
- The leadership gene pool
- Monitoring health, performance, and risk

The Right CEO and Succession

There is no more important job for the board than making sure the company has the right CEO. This means hiring and retaining the right CEO, making a good CEO better, and firing the wrong CEO. Considering that it usually takes one or two years to fully assess whether a new CEO is the right one, and another year or so for the board to come to a conclusion to replace the person, a company can suffer for years. Repeated missteps in this area are huge value destroyers.

The succession process, leading up to the selection of the right chief executive, is the single largest mechanism through which the board can add or destroy value. Boards must improve their succession and selection processes, and be prepared at all times to spring to action.

CEO Compensation

Also important is making sure that the top management team has the right compensation package. What is the philosophy or set of principles that guides the design of the package? What kinds of behaviors and actions does the board want to encourage or discourage? What is the right set of objectives to truly link pay to performance? Does the board have a framework to view the total package? Get compensation right and the CEO adds significant long-term value. Get it wrong, and a CEO could go on a debt-fuelled acquisition spree that at the extreme lands the company in bankruptcy.

The Right Strategy

Boards contribute greatly by ensuring that the company's strategy is correct for the company, the time, and the industry. One challenge is for all the directors to have the same understanding of the company's strategy. This is often lacking; different directors on the same board at times articulate vastly different versions of the company's strategy. Getting to a shared level of understanding is crucial, because strategy is an umbrella covering all of the board's work, from CEO compensation to oversight of leadership development, monitoring operating performance, and risk assessment. Directors don't develop the strategy, but their input is vital in making sure management has fully thought through its opportunities and options and has a realistic sense of the available resources, external factors, competitive threats, and risks.

The Leadership Gene Pool

The board needs to make sure that management is taking adequate steps to develop the leadership gene pool. What is the CEO succession plan? How robust is it? Do the CEO's direct reports pass muster? Does the next level of leadership have potential? How is management identifying tomorrow's leaders and how is management testing and developing them? Developing the company's leadership gene pool not only makes CEO selection easier when the time comes for succession but also ensures that business units have the best talent in the right positions. If done effectively within the context of future needs, this process provides the ultimate competitive advantage.

Monitoring Health, Performance, and Risk

Looking at earnings reports alone is not good enough for governance. The board must be forward-looking and anticipatory in making sure that the company stays financially viable at all times. Identifying and tracking the physical measures of performance underlying the financial measures further gives boards a heads-up on how plans are progressing. Many companies' grand visions dissolved because of inordinate amounts of debt taken on during good economic times. Anticipating the effect on liquidity—the availability of cash internally and externally—if risks begin to sour can change the fate of the company. Helping management identify risks and develop contingency plans if conditions don't go as expected is a tremendous contribution a board can make.

Beware of Mechanics

The many observable variables that board watchers use to assess boards of directors, such as getting the right percentage of independent directors (however defined), or splitting the CEO and Chair positions, are proxies that are only tenuously tied to good governance. Boards can't rely on them as a path to becoming Progressive. "Not everything that can be counted counts, and not everything that counts can be counted," Einstein is credited with saying, and that applies to board mechanics.

Consider one such variable: independence. The general consensus today is that most directors should be independent of the company, meaning free of financial or familial ties to the company beyond remuneration for directorship. Proponents believe that if a majority of a board's directors are independent, they will be more likely to challenge the CEO and thus to safeguard the shareholders from imperial CEOs.

The proposition is that independent directors are more likely to challenge CEOs. However, that is not necessarily the case. Many independent directors fall silent when facing strong CEOs; their lack of knowledge of the company and of its officers works against their ability to provide oversight. And many non-independent directors feel free to speak their mind.

BusinessWeek published a special report in 2003 that found that S&P 500 companies with founding families involved in management had outperformed the remainder of the S&P 500 over the preceding decade. This despite the fact that the boards of family companies tend to have a higher percentage of non-independent directors. Why? *BusinessWeek* conjectured, "With their intimate knowledge of the company gleaned from years of dinner-time conversations, many [family directors] are as knowledgeable as management about [the company's] inner workings" (November 10, 2003, p. 110). And those directors, typically with large financial stakes in the company, aren't afraid to speak up in the boardroom. They are informed and they make up a socially cohesive group. Those are some signs of Progressive boards.

This is not an argument for cronyism or nepotism in the boardroom. Far from it. The point is that personal links to a company are not very revealing of a director's contribution in the boardroom. The best directors are those who *think* independently, regardless of their status. In other words, independence is a state of mind, not a résumé item.

That's why most research on corporate governance is not very helpful. No causal relationships exist between observable variables like independence and corporate performance, so no significant correlations stand up to scrutiny. The late Sumantra Ghoshal, professor of strategy and international management at the London Business School, backed this point in a *Financial Times* comment: "The facts are clear: the proportion of independent directors on the board has absolutely no effect on corporate performance. Ditto for whether the same or different individuals occupy the posts of Chairman and Chief Executive" (September 9, 2003, p. 19).

Boards themselves know whether or not they are making a difference. Directors have to focus on the areas that really matter, regardless of whether the board watchers concur. The practices described in the coming chapters, beginning with the three building blocks in Part Two, are the key to unlocking the value of the board.

The Three Building Blocks of Progressive Boards

Understanding the differences between Liberated and Progressive boards is one thing. Making the evolutionary leap is another. To complete the transition to a Progressive board, more change is needed, and boards and CEOs themselves must drive it.

Adopting the practices and behaviors of Progressive boards creates the foundation for making substantive contributions. The following three chapters are designed to help boards overcome the problems associated with their liberation and build that foundation. The specific recommendations are battle-tested. They are based on observation of practices real boards have used to transform their work in the three areas that distinguish Progressive boards from others:

- Group dynamics
- Information architecture
- Focus on substantive issues

Chapter Three

Group Dynamics

Group dynamics underpins the board's ability to do all the components of its job—whether it's compliance and monitoring or making contributions to strategy and CEO selection. Unless individual directors can gel into a working group, they simply cannot be effective. That's why group dynamics is the first building block of a Progressive board.

Whether or not the individuals gel into an effective group is an unmistakable characteristic of a Progressive board. Every director should feel comfortable adding to the discussion. As Jeff Immelt, CEO and Chair of General Electric, says, "The boardroom has to be a place where every voice is heard. Our meetings are very open. Directors can interact with anybody, at any time." New ideas arise spontaneously as individuals build on each other's perspectives and those ideas get aired and tested by the group. Gradually, the group coalesces around a consensus view, so it may act as a single body.

Achieving that level of group dynamics is essential to becoming a Progressive board. The group dynamics can be shaped and managed by adopting practices in the following areas:

- *Rules of engagement:* Directors must together define the norms of behavior required to achieve productive dialogue.
- *Board leadership:* Boards need leaders (informal or formal) who have an innate ability to keep dialogue on track without stifling dissent, to elicit diverse views yet help the board reach consensus.
- *Executive sessions:* Executive sessions provide a forum for outside directors to air issues, but if mishandled they can be enormously damaging to the board's relationship with the CEO.

- *Board evaluation:* A board's self-evaluation should uncover the real issues that inhibit effectiveness. The directors should also be prepared to act on the important findings, individually and as a group.
- *Managing the unwanted director:* Boards must be prepared to deal with peers who are unlikely to ever become productive members of the group, or who unnecessarily drain energy from the CEO and the board.

The Rules of Engagement

Dialogue is the lifeblood of boards. It is through their incisive questioning, their debate, and their interactions with management that directors do their job. A board's contribution is made through discussions of CEO selection and succession, of the outlook for strategic initiatives, and of the management team's performance, among other topics. In the boardroom, directors must find ways to let their views be aired, to challenge one another's viewpoints if need be, without breaking the code of congeniality.

Every board has unwritten rules that guide the behavior of directors and determine the character of the dialogue. On Ceremonial boards, it's understood that directors should spend most of their time listening. On Liberated boards, directors are encouraged to speak up. But Liberated boards are discovering that while they can be very vocal, their dialogue is often not productive. Some directors give long monologues, interrupt each other to make off-topic points, or repeat the same point over and over, none of which helps the board reach conclusions or take collective action.

Progressive boards adopt rules of engagement that replace the unwritten rules of behavior that guided Ceremonial and Liberated boards. Discussions are more natural and focused than the posturing and tangents of some members of Liberated boards. Directors don't agree on everything, but they express their views candidly, debate them rigorously, and move on. The group builds on the combined experience and knowledge of the individuals.

In one executive session, a director was skeptical about a very critical initiative for the coming year. "Is it going to take too long to get the project done? Do we have enough of the right kind of people to carry this forward?" Another director recalled the timetable from previous presentations and was able to explain why she thought it was manageable. A third director explained why he thought the company's human resources would not be an impediment. Nobody from management had to defend the initiative; they weren't even in the room. The first director didn't have the knowledge base, but the other two did.

There was give-and-take in this dialogue. It was constructive and the lead director kept the discussion on track. A consensus was reached after diverse opinions were voiced and debated. When that happens, when the dialogue is a powerful eye-opener for directors and management alike, the board as a group can discharge its responsibilities.

Liberated boards can speed their evolution by airing the rules of engagement for board dialogue and interactions. The lead director or Chair of the Governance Committee might work with the CEO to generate a set of norms that can be the basis for discussion. The very process of articulating the new norms reinforces the importance of group dynamics and raises directors' awareness of how they might help or hinder the group. Even reminders to turn off cell phones and BlackBerries can be helpful; many directors comment on how often a few of their fellows can't stay focused on the meeting at hand—and how distracting it is when a director types on a BlackBerry or frequently leaves the room to take phone calls. The board doesn't have to put the rules of engagement in writing. The point is to reach a common understanding.

The board's collective judgment has to be the single most important guiding principle for the rules of engagement. Dialogue improves when directors know the rest of the board expects them to weigh in on every important topic. Getting this expectation out in the open reminds directors to speak up if they disagree with one another and to draw out a fellow director who hasn't been heard. Likewise, directors who get wrapped up in a particular point of view cannot hold the group hostage. When the board agrees to this principle, the lead director and other board members have implicit permission to solicit the views of quieter directors and to steer peers when they stray.

Productive dialogue also depends heavily on closure. Before a meeting breaks, it helps to have the lead director, Chair, or CEO (or any other director) restate the general consensus, central issues, and action items for management. The board then has the chance to hear the totality of its requests to management—and to make sure the whole board agrees that these are the most important items and that all merit attention. At this point, the board might decide to defer a few items, or to revisit certain items at subsequent meetings.

Before closing a board meeting, one CEO summarized four points. Two of the points had been made quickly by different directors at different times, but the CEO picked up on them and noted them. The directors were delighted to see how attentive the CEO was. Another two points had been missed and the board reminded the CEO of them. For example, the directors felt a presenter went on for too long and didn't have the grasp of strategy that other presenters had. The CEO agreed and pledged to coach the presenter. The process took a matter of minutes, but it reenergized the directors and began to build bonds of trust between the CEO and the non-executive directors, three of whom were new to the board.

Such closure is particularly important for executive sessions. In the end, the usefulness of an executive session is highly dependent on the communication to the CEO of the most critical issues raised. Indeed, there have been cases when a board's relationship with its CEO has been seriously strained by inaccurate or untimely feedback of an executive session's outcomes. This chapter describes several ways to improve feedback; a board should discuss what methods it will use to make sure this communication is timely and accurate.

The behavioral norms of Progressive boards eventually become routine. But for boards in transition, the norms of behavior have to be clear, well understood by all directors and the CEO, and reinforced through the board's self-evaluation and by the board's formal and informal leaders.

Board Leadership

Directors don't always want to be *led* per se—but somehow dialogue must move forward with a purpose. It must be facilitated. Not every director can effectively facilitate a board meeting. It takes a leader who has the respect of the rest of the board and the social skills to direct the flow of the discussion without offending peers or rushing to a conclusion. Many situations require a delicate social touch.

Dialogue flows in different directions all the time. In fact, directors are encouraged to explore their thoughts. Many times, another director will follow up and say, "That's a good point. Let's look at that some more," sparking a new line of inquiry. Generating those lines of inquiry and injecting a dose of skepticism is important. Mike Ruettgers, Chair and former CEO of EMC, says it might be a good idea to appoint a director to be "devil's advocate" for key decisions (such as major acquisitions) to make sure that the potential downsides of the decision are understood. "You have to make sure you see what the negatives are," he says of the practice.

Just as often, however, the other directors quickly determine that a given exploration is not a useful line of inquiry, it's a tangent. On Liberated boards, no one will interrupt the speaker. And the speaker might not be aware of going on too long, or of returning over and over to the same topic. When everyone sits quietly, it's hard to get a good read on the feeling of the group.

It takes great courage and diplomacy for a fellow director to step up and say, "It's a good point and well made. But some of us don't agree with you. Let's move on." I heard that said once by a lead director, and the group was relieved and rallied behind him. The skill is in knowing when the time for questions has passed, and in being able to redirect dialogue without stepping on anyone's toes.

There's a toughness that's required to cut someone off, and a gentleness in not breaking the code of congeniality. If the general feeling is that the individual is stuck on a non-issue, then someone— a lead director, Chair, Governance Committee Chair, or another director—must rise to the occasion and help the board move on.

Sometimes questions arise because a director lacks a full understanding of an issue. Not every director can be fully informed on every topic. For instance, there is a good chance that most directors on any given board will not fully understand derivatives. If issues arise, directors need to trust that those who do understand will ask the right questions. Other directors can remind their fellow board members not to get in the weeds on the issue.

Progressive boards rely on leaders with the special skills required to create good group dynamics. It doesn't matter whether the person who leads discussions and fosters the group dynamics is the appointed board Chair, lead director, or head of the Governance Committee. Often, leadership emerges over time, when it becomes clear that one or two directors have the skills to keep discussions on track and group dynamics positive. If that leadership is not present, the board needs to address its leadership vacuum.

Choosing the Lead Director

Boards that have lead directors typically name someone who has been on the board for a long time. In some cases, it is strictly by seniority. The logic is that these directors will have a better understanding of the company, its capabilities, and its strategy. It is also a way of honoring their contribution over many years. (The exception seems to be for a director the CEO has specifically recruited to the board to take the position, usually someone who is highly respected in the business community.)

The problem is that lead directors selected by seniority might not have the requisite skill set to lead dialogue. Progressive boards recognize the singular importance of group dynamics, so they choose the lead director who will be the best facilitator. Ideally, the lead director demonstrates several important characteristics:

- Highly respected by directors and management
- Trusted to convey feedback accurately and in a balanced manner between the board and the CEO
- Generally helpful to the CEO, though very independent
- Blessed with a knack for guiding dialogue, letting all viewpoints be heard, getting to the heart of the central issues, and keeping the discussion on track without bruising egos
- Able to keep personal ego in check

Over time, directors tend to gravitate toward those individuals who seem always able to cut to the chase. Those individuals are typically patient listeners who can process multiple viewpoints—and who sense when dialogue on a topic has ceased to be productive or needs to be energized, and have the skill to smoothly cut in. When those skills become evident, the board will know who its lead director candidates are.

Before naming a lead director, a board should take the time to discuss the realities of the job and the real capabilities required. The group should also consider the increased time commitment, which could make it difficult for sitting CEOs to take on the assignment. Some boards ask their lead directors to shoulder a greater burden in facilitating communications between management and the board between meetings, for example.

One thing boards should not consider in making appointments is the prestige factor. Nor should the position of lead director be a source of internal politicking, as happens on occasion. That behavior can damage the board's group dynamics and the relationship of the board with the CEO.

The Board and the CEO

Progressive boards maintain an open, constructive relationship with the CEO and are mindful of preserving that relationship. They recognize that the best results come from open exchanges of ideas and information. Trust is essential, as is clarity about the board's role versus the CEO's. Making explicit the role of the board and of the various positions of board leadership helps all directors understand the boundaries.

The lead director or those who hold other board positions are not there to individually challenge the CEO's power. In choosing a lead director, for example, Progressive boards define the role as that of intermediary between the board and the CEO. They look for someone who is an honest broker of information between the CEO and the board, and they are keenly aware of chemistry.

"While you can write the job description and communicate it to the board, at the end of the day, the substance of the lead director's role is determined by the chemistry between the Lead Director and the CEO," says Jack Krol, Lead Director of Tyco, director at MeadWestvaco and Ace Insurance, former CEO and Chair of DuPont, and NACD Director of the Year in 1998.

At Tyco, Krol and Ed Breen (CEO and Chair) have explicitly worked out the division of responsibilities, as illustrated in Exhibit 3.1, and the role has evolved as the company's situation has changed. Every company is different, of course, and Tyco faced the unique situation of rebuilding its board in the aftermath of the scandals.

Other boards have to spend time working out their own version of this chart, and would probably consider different divisions of roles. However, the process of putting them on paper can be enormously helpful to the group dynamics.

"I think we've defined the roles pretty well per the document," says Breen. "To me, though, what has worked well are some of the softer issues. As much as Jack is involved, what he doesn't do is get involved in the operations of the company and try to make any of those decisions. It is very clear in the company that he's not going to do that." So managers and directors alike all understand that when Krol and the other directors visit field offices, as they periodically do, they are not there to micromanage.

Krol took on enormous responsibility in the revamping of Tyco's corporate governance. Not all directors have the time available to tackle such a workload. Some boards rotate key positions, such as lead director. In part, this is done to share the workload. Other boards do this with an eye to avoid creating a concentration of power, perceived or real, on the board. But this practice can also prevent the lead director from forming a constructive relationship with the CEO. It's a judgment call whether a board should adopt this practice. They should be wary, though, of one-year rotations. One year sounds like a long time, but since boards typically have six or eight meetings per year, it might not be long enough for relationships to develop. Three years is probably more reasonable.

Executive Sessions

Now required by several stock exchanges, executive sessions can be a powerful tool for transforming the board's group dynamics. But the mere assemblage of outside directors without management present does not necessarily equate with good governance. Done poorly, executive sessions can create destructive rifts and undermine an otherwise competent management. Thus executive sessions must be handled with care.

With few precedents to guide behaviors and outcomes, directors are often unsure what to do and say. Some directors believe executive sessions a waste of time, and some CEOs feel threatened by them. Executive sessions can arouse suspicion and distrust when there is a perception that every session is an impromptu performance

**Exhibit 3.1. Roles of the Chair/CEO
and Lead Director at Tyco.**

Chair/CEO

- Leads board meetings
- Builds positive working relationship with the board
- Strives for constructive, effective, value-added, focused meetings
- Ensures focus on the right issues and provides useful information
- Keeps board informed on a timely basis of significant positives/negatives (totally open and honest)
- Uses meetings and other contacts with board to tap knowledge and wisdom
- Strives to make the board a competitive advantage
- Provides board open access to senior management team

Lead Director

- Ongoing communication with CEO—messages from board (other board members also encouraged to communicate)
- Leads Executive Sessions of board and provides prompt and candid feedback to CEO
- Obtains board members' and management's input and sets board agenda (with CEO)
- Works with CEO to get right flow of information to the board on a timely basis
- Facilitates communications among directors
- Partners with and coaches CEO (help make CEO successful)
- Stays current on major risks; focuses board on these
- Molds a cohesive board to support success of CEO
- Assists in recruiting effort for new board members (with Nominating & Governance Committee and CEO)
- Ensures governance processes are leading edge (with Nominating & Governance Committee and CEO)
- CEO discussion (with Chair of Compensation Committee) on a) Personal development discussion; b) Compensation

Source: Ty

review. But conducting executive sessions routinely not only reduces that perception but also prevents situations from becoming extreme. To further counter these perceptions, Progressive boards determine ahead of time what the rules of the road will be for these sessions—who will conduct them, what topics will be discussed, which topics are off limits, and how the executive session will link management with the board.

The greatest value of executive sessions is that by lowering the hurdles for asking questions and expressing opinions and instincts, they give directors a chance to test their thoughts and insights among their peers. As they bring their thoughts to the surface, directors can find out what their peers are picking up and whether there are areas that need to be explored. By creating a candid and trusting atmosphere, directors can air their concerns before they become too acute and without sounding threatening. The goal of the executive session, then, should be to get ideas and insights on the table and determine as a group which to pursue further.

The selection of topics is very important. Some boards solicit directors for agenda items before the executive session. Initially, an agenda might even include discussion of the rules of the road for the sessions. But Progressive boards generally find a tight agenda too restrictive. They prefer to keep the sessions more informal, allowing the free flow of ideas and topics—but keeping a careful ear on the dialogue to make sure no thread goes on too long if it is not a weighty issue.

The boundaries for discussions should be defined up front. There might be a few standing questions. One board has its Governance Committee Chair ask during each meeting, "Is there anything that we think should be a board meeting agenda item in the future?" Not every issue that is raised will make it onto the agenda. A director, for example, suggested that the agenda include supply chain issues in China. After discussion, the board came to a full consensus that the issue didn't have a high enough priority for a boardroom discussion. Having the forum to suggest the agenda item made it clear that every director had some input on the agenda, and no director, not even the one who suggested the supply chain topic, felt shut out. He was able to test his thinking and see how the other directors felt.

Other appropriate topics could include impressions of a presenter's potential abilities or the quality of information given to the board. Sometimes it's helpful to test observations like "the CEO's focus seems diluted" or "turnover among senior executives has been awfully high," to see if other directors are picking up on the same signals. Those intuitions often lead to spirited discussions and substantive feedback to the CEO.

In one executive session, directors asked whether the company was growing too quickly. "According to this strategy, this business is really going to grow in size and complexity," a director observed, to which a second director asked, "Do we have the capability to handle that growth?" They spent forty minutes discussing it, and the lead director called on each board member to gather all perspectives. The board began to focus on two aspects of this growth: How will processes have to change to manage the size? Does the company have the people to make this growth happen? In the end, they concurred that they should ask the CEO to take the board through a three-year plan of the organization's people and processes.

On the other hand, to be avoided are discussions in which the CEO's knowledge and presence are important, or topics that could easily lead the outside directors to form a premature conclusion. Directors should avoid, for instance, deciding for or against an acquisition in executive session, or even going too deeply into that discussion without the CEO. Management will have important insights or knowledge that would shape opinions or contradict other points that are being raised. Non-executive directors might instead conclude that they are not satisfied with the rationale for an acquisition and perhaps put together a set of questions to be discussed with management.

Executive Sessions and Management

Executive sessions are held without the CEO, but it's important to understand that management is still involved. In fact, the value of the executive session can only be realized when there is effective communication with management. This is relevant both before and after a session.

One practice that works is to have the CEO present at the start to answer questions. The Q&A sets the stage for the executive session and gives the CEO a chance to see where the board is going. Many questions that directors have can be answered only by the CEO or the management team.

Directors must take care, of course, to phrase their questions in a way that doesn't make the CEO defensive. For example, a comment such as "I don't think we are being very aggressive in pricing" could be turned into a reasonable question: "I'd like to learn about how pricing in the industry will change given inflationary pressure in commodities, and how our margins are being affected. What tools and techniques are we using for pricing to cope with the pressures?"

Even more important is what happens after the executive session. The gist of the discussion should be communicated to the CEO in a constructive manner that enables action. As the executive session winds to a close, the board must be aware of what it needs to tell the CEO. Directors must spend time to articulate their views of the most important topics, select the questions they would like answered or addressed for the next meeting, and agree on what the CEO will be told. On some boards, the lead director will restate the consensus opinion on what to communicate to the CEO.

Determining what is constructive and what the CEO might perceive as a cheap shot, an impression that is sometimes conveyed unintentionally, tests the board's maturity. The temptation is to be comprehensive in telling the CEO every point that came up. But boards should be selective about what they tell the CEO, particularly regarding personal performance. Be thoughtful, skip the minor points, and don't give more than one or two items of feedback for personal improvement at a time.

Finally, the person presiding over the executive session plays an important role in delivering the CEO feedback. The accuracy and honesty of this feedback are crucial. These are delicate matters. The wrong choice of words, the wrong tone, or any insensitivity can be very detrimental. Even if it's a criticism, make it constructive—not sugar-coated, but not unnecessarily harsh. The vast majority of leaders welcome the help. More often, the feedback is merely a request or concern.

CEOs often suspect that they are not being told the whole truth. One CEO heard from his lead director after an executive session, but got a different story over dinner with a good friend on the board. He wondered if the lead director deliberately withheld information because there was an ulterior motive, or whether he was just a poor communicator. Boards should be careful to reduce such suspicions and avoid misunderstandings.

Some Progressive boards make sure that two directors give the feedback together. This practice allows them to cross-check with each other what nuances of the dialogue to convey, and it validates the overall feedback for the CEO.

Other Progressive boards have the CEO reenter the room while the whole board is still present. The lead director summarizes for the CEO what was discussed in the executive session. This practice also creates an opportunity for all the directors to see and hear the CEO's reaction to the feedback. Is it being received as intended? Is the recipient clamming up and becoming defensive? Most CEOs are appreciative of this type of immediate feedback and it will show in their body language. The areas in which CEOs appear hesitant are areas for the board to watch.

Of course, the board should expect follow-through on the feedback. For example, during one executive session, directors began to question the quality of a few very senior officers compared to their counterparts at a competitor, so they asked the CEO, "How are you evaluating these people?" At the next board meeting, the CEO provided more information and launched a discussion on the potential people problem. Directors began to see more of the picture, and they collectively changed their minds.

If feedback is not provided right after the session, it should be conveyed within a day or two, so that the discussion is fresh in directors' minds. And under no circumstances should comments or feedback be attributed to individual directors. Continued confidentiality is of utmost importance. There is nothing wrong with encouraging an individual director to talk to the CEO directly if it will be of help, but the comments should never be relayed on a name basis. Confidentiality helps improve the candor of the dialogue.

Board Evaluation

It's now a listing requirement of the NYSE that boards, along with their Nominating, Governance, Compensation, and Audit Committees, all perform annual evaluations. But Progressive boards have known all along that self-evaluation is a vital process—one that ensures continuous improvement and renewal. The external environment is ever changing and the board must be prepared to change with it. There is always room to improve.

Progressive boards not only spend time designing robust processes for board and committee improvement, they also give weight to individual director assessments. Bringing up the issue of individual assessments can be awkward. Directors are often uncomfortable with the idea of evaluating each other.

The reluctance to have a peer evaluation process is understandable. But if individual assessments are well done, they can be enormously powerful without breaking the code of congeniality. Individual assessments aren't intended to generate performance grades. They simply identify how directors can be more effective.

Some feel they are unqualified to evaluate the Warren Buffetts of the world. But the best directors want that feedback. They want to know how they are enhancing the group—or not. Great directors didn't get where they are without being sensitive and responsive to constructive feedback from peers.

Boards that have gotten past their initial skepticism are enthusiastic about evaluating individual board members. When one director received some positive feedback on how his colleagues valued what he said, it encouraged him to participate more. A different director was often seen doing calculations during presentations and his questions were considered nitpicky. It was difficult to give this director critical feedback, because he was a respected CEO at a prominent company. But when he heard from his colleagues, he pledged to do better. The process allowed him to receive this feedback without putting him on the defensive. It made the feedback more palatable and indeed, he acted upon it.

Unfortunately, Liberated boards' self-evaluations rarely get to the real issues underlying the board's effectiveness. Some boards think the idea of a "formal evaluation" means a survey with check-lists and tick boxes that can be captured numerically. They ask general questions that don't result in steps that lead to action.

Progressive boards use informal interviews by a third-party interviewer who reports back to the Chair, lead director, or head of the Governance Committee. These one-on-one interviews get directors engaged and yield far more candid responses than do written surveys and checklists with set options, provided the evaluator is someone who has good judgment, is highly trusted, and has a good sense of the company, the industry, and the individuals.

The questions should be forward-looking and lead to insights for self-improvement. They should be open-ended enough to begin new dialogues about the workings of the board, rather than closed and designed to produce ratings and conclusions that don't suggest any action steps. The questions are not designed to trap directors into making critical remarks or pointing fingers at one another, but rather to open an exchange between the interviewer and the director about what the board does well and how the board can improve. The evaluator shouldn't let any directors off the hook without making at least one concrete suggestion.

For the board evaluation, for example, an interviewer might begin by asking a director, "On a scale of 1 to 10, how relevant is the board's Twelve-Month Agenda?" If a director responds with a rating of 6, follow-up questions emerge: "What could be done to improve that rating?" for example. "What elements are missing from the agenda?" These nuances reveal potential improvements in both substance and process.

The General Electric board, already one of the best and most Progressive, used a best-in-class interview-based process for board evaluation in 2003. The findings led to a set of precise action items, including these key steps among them:

- Spend more time understanding one division at an important strategic juncture.
- Over time, keep on the lookout for potential directors whose experience could enhance the board in the future.
- Have committees spend more time informing the board of the full thinking behind their recommendations.

- Have the CEO meet with non-executive directors without inside directors present.
- Increase the use of a specific practice for issues requiring in-depth discussion. Breaking into groups of three or four directors for deliberation and then bringing the full board back together for more dialogue brings out the best of the board.
- From time to time, have management update the board on how well major acquisitions are proceeding against forecasts made at the time of approval.

For peer evaluations, an interviewer would ask each director about the rest of the board. If this is done well, directors open up with brief but candid responses that wouldn't come out in a written survey. After the interviews are complete, it usually becomes clear that there are one or two things that some directors might do more of, or might do less of, to make the group more effective. The skill of the interviewer is in exercising good judgment in compiling the core thoughts about each director.

The evaluation process should be sure to include questions having to do with leadership of the board. Are the Chair, lead director, and committee Chairs getting the group focused on the right issues? Keeping the quality of dialogue high? Helping the group reach consensus?

Finally, the findings should be captured, the minutiae filtered out, and recommendations made to the board. The idea is to identify the central themes and concrete suggestions, and then leave it to the board, led by the Governance Committee Chair or the lead director, to conduct a discussion of the results. The board itself can then conclude with a set of action steps and follow-through. The head of the Governance Committee should make sure there's full agreement on the recommendations, and then monitor the follow-through over time.

This process can be repeated every year. When it is annual, directors will become accustomed to making small changes in behavior over time and will know they have the opportunity to be recognized for their improvements. It is better to make a series of small midcourse corrections than attempt to make major changes every three years.

Managing the Unwanted Director

As directors become more cognizant of the importance of group dynamics, they are taking a close look at individual directors' contributions to that dynamic. Unfortunately, some boards realize that there are times in which they have to deal with directors who hijack dialogue and poison the group's interactions. Occasionally, a director doesn't pick up on the signals that this kind of behavior is detracting from the group dynamics. An "unwanted" director can single-handedly derail the board's group dynamics and create an enormous time sink for a board and a CEO. A board needs to deal with this problem, because it will not go away on its own.

There is an important distinction to be made here between a *dissenting* director and an *unwanted* director. Debate in the boardroom should be encouraged, and that means making sure that dissenting opinions are heard. Dissenting directors know how to disagree without being disagreeable. They understand where a board's consensus is headed and are respectful of the board's collective opinion. They may be outspoken, but they are willing to rethink issues as more viewpoints are heard. They also understand the importance of time pressure and make a conscious effort not to dominate the board's agenda.

In short, dissenting directors, however outspoken, are respected contributors. And while some fellow directors or management may lack the patience to hear them out and may want to railroad the discussion, these directors should be heard. Indeed, letting them lay out their entire thought process is the best way for the board to ensure that it's not missing something and for the dissenters to ultimately accept the results when the consensus goes against them.

Unwanted directors are a different breed. These directors ask academic questions or are full of non sequiturs. They ask for too much granularity or too much generality. Sometimes they pontificate on their own experiences, seemingly to demonstrate how smart they are. One director would literally pull out his calculator to search for inconsistencies in the financial reports and would stop the discussion in its tracks if he found something.

It's not just what they talk about, though. It's also how they talk that makes them unwanted. Unwanted directors will continually push dialogue down rabbit holes and repeatedly ask the same questions. They rarely sense that the other directors do not agree with them. I've seen board members roll their eyes or stare at their shoes when these unwanted directors start speaking. Unwanted directors have lost the respect of their peers.

When unwanted directors go off on a tangent, the remainder of the board has a responsibility to rein them in. The CEO can't stop the questioning because that will seem defensive. Thus fellow directors must step up; they must respectfully redirect the dialogue or else it becomes impossible for the board to get anything done. It's not just the lead director's responsibility. If more directors speak up, it will become more evident that the weight of dialogue has shifted away from the unwanted director.

When these remedies are not enough, however, some boards go further. They give the lead director or Chair of the Governance Committee support in dealing one-on-one with directors who are disruptive. This could spur an offline conversation about the rules of engagement. In the extreme, the Nominating Committee could decide to not renominate the unwanted director.

To preserve group dynamics, Progressive boards face up to this uncomfortable situation and withstand the consequences. Directors who are pushed out can become disgruntled. A few directors have even become vindictive. In one case, when an unwanted director was told he would not be renominated, he abruptly resigned and made public his disagreements with the board's policies and decisions. Whether his arguments were weighty or not, the director should have realized that he needed to work within the dynamics of the board to change his peers' minds. Resigning and making public allegations rarely do any good for the company or the individuals involved.

| **Information Architecture**

Good group dynamics are not much use when directors lack information for a productive discussion. The bottom line: Boards need the right information in the right format at the right time.

Unfortunately, Liberated boards often find the quantity, substance, or format of information they receive to be inadequate. Worse, directors on the same board often have different views on what information is desirable—some want more; some want less. What they can agree on is that the information often falls short in helping them build any insights into the business.

Whether it's spreadsheets of raw accounting data, reports filled with company jargon, thick books of information sent too close to the board meeting to be fully understood, or scripted PowerPoint presentations made during board meetings, the information Liberated boards receive does little to ensure good oversight, let alone prepare directors for meaty discussions on important topics. Meeting time is too often spent regurgitating or deciphering the information rather than drawing out directors' insights and judgments.

On Liberated boards, several directors might make personal requests for more information, bordering on the unreasonable. On one board, two directors had an insatiable appetite for information. They kept asking the CEO for more detail or different measures. In the spirit of breaking from the Ceremonial past, the CEO and his team spent a tremendous amount of time addressing the directors' inquiries, most of which other board members felt were not relevant to the board's work. It's not uncommon for CEOs to respond to repeated requests for information by inundating the board with reports.

The net effect is corrosive to group dynamics. If the board is saddled with an overload of reports, it loses focus on the important issues. If directors lack enough detail to formulate questions, the dialogue suffers and devolves into a review of financials. If management scrambles to respond to ad hoc requests by individual directors, it burns valuable time.

Boards cannot evolve until they address the information flow. Both the board and management benefit when they get on the same page regarding what information the board needs, when, and how it should be conveyed. When information is well architected, the board can focus on ideas rather than on the information itself. And packaging the information the board is looking for often helps management diagnose and detect problems sooner.

Information also builds trust. "The day a company does not operate with the full trust of its board is the day a company ceases to exist. And trust is an indicator of information flow. So we have to be completely open with, and transparent to, our board," says Jeff Immelt, CEO and Chair of General Electric.

Building the foundation for productive discussions begins by getting the board (or a few members) to work with management to design the information architecture.

Designing the Information Architecture

Information architecture describes all of the ways the board gets information, whether it's communications from management in preparation for board meetings or planned visits by directors to company sites. It specifies what kinds of information the board will get when, and in what format.

Think of information architecture as having a number of channels that directors tune in to at different times, for different reasons. Every board will have to design with management its own particular information architecture, but Progressive boards find the following channels to be especially useful:

- *Channel 1—Board Briefing:* A succinct report that captures the current state of affairs with no jargon, to prepare directors before each board meeting.

- *Channel 2—Management Letter:* A short topical letter or communication from the CEO that keeps directors abreast of current conditions within and outside the company between meetings.
- *Channel 3—Employee Survey:* A periodic instrument the board can request from management to monitor a specific set of issues.
- *Channel 4—Director Outreach:* The commitment of time to visit stores or plants, speak directly with line managers, attend conferences, and otherwise experience the business firsthand.
- *Channel 5—Reports from Committees:* Recommendations and relevant background information presented to the full board.

A board's information architecture specifies the kind of information each channel will convey. The information directors need most is a commonsense look at how money is made in the business over the long and short term, measures that show whether the company is progressing or deteriorating relative to the external environment, and subjective information that reveals the assumptions and conceptual thinking underlying management's proposals and decisions.

Other information directors need is more forward-looking, helping the board ensure a leadership pipeline, become comfortable with the company's and the operating units' strategies, or understand and anticipate the risks associated with taking the company in a certain direction. Once those needs are sharply defined, it's relatively easy to figure out how to package and present the information to make it clear and concise.

Information must still be exchanged informally through dialogue inside and outside the boardroom. For Ceremonial boards, contact between executives and directors outside the boardroom was taboo, but today informal conversations between directors or between management and individual directors is common. CEOs have long sought out directors for input on issues for which the director has particular expertise, Washington experience, for example, or to follow up on an issue that the director raised in a meeting. But directors also should feel free to ask the CEO's direct reports for information, taking care not to overstep their bounds. Sometimes a brief one-on-one conversation with a division head is all that's needed for a director to fill in gaps in understanding.

Informal contact with leaders below the CEO gives directors the opportunity to gain many insights into the business. As Bob Weissman, director at Pitney Bowes and former CEO of IMS Health, Cognizant, and Dun & Bradstreet, says, "When it comes to strategy, this kind of contact gives me a lot more insight about what's going on in the organization, in the marketplace, and with competitors and customers than I would ever get by just listening to a PowerPoint presentation in a board meeting. On compliance, if you think about how a board member uncovers noncompliance, you realize that you have to rely on people who observe it, the management, to tell you. They'll only tell you if they trust you."

Channel 1—Board Briefing

In Progressive companies, management replaces the typical thick binder of information with a package covering a range of business, legal, people, industry, and economic issues to help the board see the big picture. Anything that is material to the business should be in this board briefing. But while a board briefing includes much of the relevant financial information that directors are accustomed to receiving, it also includes a few pages of management's commentary on the most relevant categories of information.

As an example, here is a summary of one company's board briefing. The package, distributed a week before a board meeting, contained information and commentary in four major categories:

- Financial and performance information, including projections for the year, broken out by business unit. This took up almost twenty pages. However, it was prefaced by a single introductory page that led directors to the high points. This section made it easy for directors to penetrate the data and prompted them to raise some questions about the nature of operating cash flow trends.
- A five-page report from the CEO and the senior vice president of human relations. The idea was to engage the board on a proposed change in organizational structure. The report was succinct and analytical. Because the briefing mapped out alternatives as well as the pros and cons of the change, directors

didn't have to spend their time bringing them to the surface; they could spend their time debating the change.

- A package of material involving Sarbanes-Oxley provisions. It included three outside opinions on issues related to the law and NYSE requirements. Here, management overlooked an opportunity to include its own views on which points were most directly relevant. Still, including the information in the board briefing helped the board focus on the nuances of the legislation.
- The consent agenda of routine compliance items. This included which individuals were reappointed as officers, and a discussion of salary raises across the company. Directors could review the list ahead of time and not waste meeting time going through items that didn't warrant discussion.

It's important to note that the financial and performance information, the first category of the board briefing, differs from what Liberated boards are used to. The key is to simplify the business and get to the fundamentals. Several ingredients are a must. First, a comprehensive review of cash flows is required. Where is cash going, business by business? Where is cash coming from? How is cash allocated and why?

Cash flow is among the best measures of a company's historical performance, present condition, and future capabilities. Some boards might look at cash generation and cash usage to see how well the match creates shareholder value. Other boards focus on debt obligations. They don't want to find themselves in charge of the next Vivendi, letting liquidity problems become acute in adverse economic conditions.

The second essential ingredient is a set of performance indicators (a fuller discussion of performance indicators is in Chapter Ten), which are useful for management also. These are the real, physical measures that lead to financial outcomes; they capture the link between customers and cash flow. While many boards scrutinize gross margin, for example, few systematically measure what is happening in the business to drive margins. A bookstore chain, for example, would watch the mix between low-margin product categories such as recorded music and high-margin categories such as cafés. Other companies might watch for changes in competitors' pricing, or unforeseen changes in commodities prices.

By focusing on the drivers, directors can spot problems sooner and use their collective expertise to ensure that management is properly addressing what is happening. This practice also gets management to spot problems and opportunities—often before the information even gets to the board. The format makes management more vigilant and more effective.

Including a few external measures of where the industry is going and benchmarks against competitors gives directors a clear picture of the evolving competitive environment. Market share information is helpful, but it needs to be supplemented with the reasons for improvement or decline. Information is also needed on how cost structure and margins are going to shift over the next few years by product line, customer segment, or distribution channel, relative to anticipated competitors' moves.

Different companies need to identify the unique set of measures that pertain to them. Companies with a heavy concentration on a few customers with large contracts, for example, might include in their board briefings the anatomy of those contracts and measures of how well they are being executed, so the board can assess risk. Companies in the pharmaceutical industry might look at the timing and speed with which the market for a patented drug shifts to generics.

High-tech product companies with multigenerational products, such as semiconductor manufacturers, might put in their board briefing technology maps that show how particular technologies link to different market segments and what the pricing, cost, and demand structures are in those segments. Management needs to inform the board of any significant changes in competitors' segmentation, as well, including the creation of new segments.

A third ingredient shows how the company is deploying its resources. The most obvious place to start is to look at budget priorities and capital investment. But just as important is for the board to get a sense for human resources, and particularly the leadership gene pool. How is the roster of up-and-coming leaders changing? How are they being developed?

Finally, there are reports from third-party sources of information—equity analysts, ratings agencies, market research firms, and so on. Directors should regularly monitor these to understand how the company is viewed by capital markets and by customers. There are times when analysts raise red flags—debt covenants that accentuate risk, for example, or declining brand equity—that must be brought up for discussion. In the late 1990s, for example, an analyst wrote a report bluntly asserting that Compaq had reached a point relative to Dell that it had to either cut its prices and let its margins suffer, or lose market share and maintain its margins. He served notice that Dell, still much smaller than Compaq at the time, was driving competition. That sort of analysis should be brought to the attention of a board.

Analysts, for all their faults, do have financial models. They do collect competitive information. Some even interview and conduct focus groups of customers. But reports from buy-side analysts amount to a considerable tonnage, enough so that directors couldn't possibly keep up on their own. So management should package together what the analysts are saying, along with the underlying reasoning behind both the good and the bad. Management could produce these summaries every three months for the board. These sources may not always be right, but if their opinions carry weight among customers and investors, then their conclusions should be given consideration.

Management's commentary can be an important part of a board briefing. The practice should be discussed ahead of time by the CEO and the board, to ensure that management will commit the time to produce thoughtful and accurate commentary and the board will trust that management is capturing the high points. Although it takes time for management to think through and produce the commentary, many chief executives have told me it is time well spent. When management writes in plain English, with no acronyms or buzzwords, it helps the board grasp the crucial facts, trends, and ideas.

It is particularly important to include management commentary for financial data. The commentary gets directors' mental wheels turning so they don't have to distill hundreds of pages of financial data. Then, when CEOs kick-off board meetings with a financial review, they can replace the mind-numbing line-by-line review of the numbers with a simple opening statement that leads right to substantive dialogue: "Let's discuss your thoughts, concerns, and questions regarding performance." The time required to review financials at the start of a meeting can be cut by 50 percent or more.

Management's commentary must be perfectly candid at all times. For example, at Banco Popular, a leading financial institution in Puerto Rico, management led off with the bad news—that two global powerhouses were moving into Banco Popular's major product category—and with the steps the bank would take to protect its position. The threat was clearly stated up front and not sugar-coated, so directors could focus their attention immediately on the issues where management needed their input.

The board briefing format is designed jointly by the board and management. One company had its lead director work with the CEO and the CFO. Other companies have the Governance Committee or the Audit Committee sit with the management team. Use an ad hoc temporary committee formed specifically for this purpose if need be. Once the basic format is agreed on, the board briefing should remain roughly the same for every meeting. This creates consistency and clarity and helps the board see changes to the company and its performance over time.

Channel 2—Management Letter

Months might pass between board meetings, yet business goes on 365 days per year. The competitive landscape is continuously changing. Directors can't be expected to live and breathe the company in the way that senior managers do. They may not be able to stay abreast of all the latest developments within the company or of news events and trends that could affect the company.

Thus boards should request that their CEOs establish a way to keep them informed between board meetings. Even boards that meet eight times per year need to make sure there is some communication during the months when a meeting is not scheduled. A simple letter from the CEO to directors is a surprisingly useful tool.

The approach is simple: In the past thirty days, what are the three or four top-of-mind items that directors should know about? The most important thing a CEO can provide is bad news. Perhaps a legal issue is overhanging the company, or a key customer was lost. Perhaps a competitor has made an acquisition or an important manager has stepped down.

The next most important is current information that is relevant to the business, presented in a way that provides some context and gives the CEO's perspective. For example, if a question was raised in a board meeting about how well a particular distribution channel was accepting a new product line, the CEO could send a short letter describing how the product line is progressing. This keeps the issue alive and provides continuity. A CEO might inform the board about major FDA, FCC, or FTC decisions and how they might affect the company's plans. Or changes to a particular industry structure, the impact of an emerging technology, a response to a story in the media, or an update on a direct report.

Boards also need to be informed of emerging issues involving the range of constituencies that make demands on the corporation. Retirees have an interest in how the pension plan is operated; employees have an interest in compensation and benefits policies; communities have an interest in globalization and the transfer of jobs; nations have an interest in environmental impacts; the list goes on.

A third set of information relates to issues that are likely to emerge in the next couple of months—a potential merger in the industry, for example, or a bill pending in Congress. Giving directors a heads-up helps them focus their attention and gives them insight into how the CEO is tracking and interpreting the landscape.

Ivan Seidenberg, CEO and Chairman of Verizon, uses a different approach to keep the board informed and up to speed in the fast-changing telecom industry. He blocks off time at every meeting to orally update the board on his personal and informal view of three or four aspects of the changing external environment that could affect the industry or the company. "We try to get ahead of the learning curve," he says of the technique. He also sends a management letter when meetings are more spaced out, signaling what is likely to come in the meeting ahead. The topics are always high-level and, for the most part, unrelated to specific decisions that needed to be made.

The management letter, as Seidenberg shows, can take more than one form. Sometimes e-mail will suffice, or a conference call. In fact, many companies are building board Web sites to distribute information to directors more efficiently, and to foster improved communications. Reports can be downloaded as desired by a director.

Web sites, intranets, and e-mail have great potential for the board's information architecture—and even its group dynamics.

Communication skills are important. If the letter is in writing, the text should be concise, interesting, and to the point. If it's oral, the statements should be brief, informal, and open-ended. Whatever the delivery vehicle, directors should be kept in the know regularly, not only to inform them of the latest developments but also to keep them thinking about the company.

Don't let a CEO feel that directors will not devote time to these thought pieces. Directors on Progressive boards love to dig in on strategic issues. By engaging them with forward-looking, thoughtful, and timely communications, CEOs can keep the company's central issues at the top of directors' minds, ensuring deeper discussions, more efficient use of meeting time, and better continuity from meeting to meeting. Directors' insights outside the boardroom can also add a lot of value.

Channel 3—Employee Surveys

Boards have an obligation to understand the company at levels beyond the executive suite. That means reaching out to employees.

One device that's proved effective is the employee survey, which can be targeted at specific topics of importance to the company and to the board. Boards can request that management initiate surveys to assess very specific issues, for example, the culture of the company, or how well the code of conduct is practiced in the company. Management can then engage a third-party firm to conduct the actual data gathering and analysis.

After one major acquisition, for example, a company needed to combine two very different cultures. A smooth integration was crucial to meeting the financial expectations that underpinned the acquisition. But waiting for the financial measures to be reported guaranteed a delay before the board knew how the integration was proceeding. The directors wanted something more direct to tell them how well it was working out.

Knowing that the integration issues would be played out below the executive suite, the board went straight to the source. The directors had management work with a third party to design an online survey distributed to the top one hundred managers at the combined company. The survey was carefully designed to unearth potential roadblocks to creating a unified company, particularly whether managers thought the processes for making resource allocation decisions and for evaluating managers were fair. Some questions were multiple choice but others were open-ended, to allow individuals to anonymously raise any issues the survey designers might have overlooked.

From the survey results, it was clear that the integration was proceeding very well, though decision making in one business unit was still ambiguous, and the criteria for resource allocation were not yet fully ironed out. Open-ended comments were also very candid. The survey results gave the board direction on which areas to ask management about in forthcoming meetings. It further reassured the board that the CEO was on the right track. And management was able to focus its attention on areas to accelerate the integration process itself.

Channel 4—Director Outreach

To truly put their fingers on the pulse of the company, directors on Progressive boards schedule face time with employees, division managers, customers, and suppliers. Through personal interactions directors get a much better sense for customer service, internal culture, and the company's value proposition.

As one step, boards should consider having directors make regular site visits to manufacturing plants, retail outlets, or satellite offices to get a feel for what the business is, who the people are who work there, who the customers are, and how customers think of the company. Not all directors have the time for regular visits to every office, store, or plant. But it's a good practice for some, if not all, directors to stop in every once in a while. Home Depot directors, for example, are required to visit stores between scheduled board meetings. GE and Intel directors visit plant sites every year.

Directors should have a sense for how the company works and of the customer experience at a hands-on level, not just a conceptual level. At Rohm and Haas, four to five board members meet with senior management without the CEO or COO present to get a sense for what is really happening in the company, as well as to have an opportunity to assess talent for succession. At the same time, they always ask, "What can we, as directors, do to help you out?" It's an invaluable practice not only for the board but also for the senior executives.

Directors may have different opinions as to how many visits to make and how long the visits should be. The board should debate the appropriate engagement and revisit it periodically. At one company, the lead director makes a point of visiting at least one business unit per quarter and invites other directors to come with him. It provides an opportunity to meet with various business teams and hear about the different businesses firsthand. "At the same time," the lead director explains, "I probe what the risks are in each business."

On one such visit to an overseas operation, he realized that they supplied industrial companies throughout Europe from just one warehouse. He says, "'What if it burned down?' I thought, 'All of a sudden, you'd shut down an entire industry across the continent.' That's the kind of thing that doesn't come out unless you go out in the field and start asking field managers questions. To them, it was no big deal, a fact of life. To me, that was an important thing we had to think about." The visit prompted an insight that he then raised with management.

This lead director makes it clear during his visits that he is not there to micromanage, and he typically gets a positive response from field managers. He gets a chance to learn about the businesses, to get to know key leaders, and people in the field get a sense of what the board is thinking about. He says, "They're always curious about what the board thinks, and I'm happy to talk to them about it."

At Intel, Reed Hundt and his fellow directors visit many Intel sites, as *Fortune* magazine wrote on August 23, 2004. Hundt might engage with the firm's engineers to learn about technologies. But just like the lead director at the firm described earlier, he also fields questions, comments, and complaints about whatever issues are on the mind of the rank-and-file staff. He can not only experience the culture of the company firsthand but also communicate his insights and intuitions back to top management.

Visits don't need to be formally announced and scheduled. In some cases, directors can simply swing by a store or an office. Whatever directors pick up as critical issues should be brought back to the boardroom in the form of incisive observations and productive questions.

Internal and external auditors are also important information sources, as most Audit Committees know. Strengthening informal communication with internal auditors helps open that channel. One proactive Audit Committee Chair told me that her committee comes to board meetings a day early specifically to spend half a day with line managers such as the firm's buyers, because they are the ones who drive many accounting issues. The frequent meetings create familiarity and make the staff more comfortable communicating with committee members. These are the techniques that Progressive boards use to make sure they truly understand the company and its people.

Channel 5—Reports from Committees

Directors must be deeply informed on critical topics, but not every director is expected to have the same depth of knowledge on every issue. The work of the board needs to be divided, which is why the board has committees. Board committees play two vital roles: the first is to dig into complex subject matter, and the second is to keep the rest of the board up to speed in those areas. Boards need to explicitly consider how their committees will report to the full board.

Committees bring recommendations to the full board, but the full board is the true decision maker. Take the Compensation Committee. With all the public scrutiny placed on pay packages, it is very important for each and every director to fully understand the payout as well as the philosophy behind the package and the process of defining it. If they don't, they could wind up in court. There have to be clear mechanisms for committees and their heads to present the most important recommendations and the reasoning behind them to the full board—and the full board to have ample discussion before a decision is made.

While it's important to make sure the entire board debates and understands crucial issues underlying committees' work, some of the nitty-gritty work could be kept within the committee. *Fortune* magazine detailed how Intel delegates compliance work to its committees. "Each director, of course, has to sign off on the audit review and compensation plan each year," *Fortune* wrote, "but the full board now devotes less time to reviewing committee work" (August 23, 2004, p. 76). There has to be trust in the judgment of the directors on each committee.

Many boards are experiencing, in one director's words, tension over the need for information that would once have been the domain of the committees. That is, in some cases, directors are requesting so much information on committee deliberations that the committee work is simply repeated in the board meeting. To reduce this tension, one board invites all directors to sit in on all committee meetings, to be open and inclusive for the more curious of the directors.

Setting aside ample time for the board to debrief the committees goes a long way in dissipating directors' worries and making the board more efficient. The committees should summarize key facts and crystallize the issues and recommendations ahead of time. The Chairs might even consider preparing a report similar to the board briefing ahead of scheduled discussions.

| **Focus on Substantive Issues**

Often, directors and CEOs feel stymied, sensing that they are not devoting enough time to the topics and issues that really matter. As one experienced director observed, "Most boards use up their meeting time on two things: one is listening to last quarter's results, dissected in unnecessarily minute detail with very little focus on the future, and the other is watching the 'dog and pony' shows put on by operating people." Too often, discussions of important matters such as strategy, succession, and external trends are squeezed in around the edges, leaving directors and CEOs dissatisfied and opportunities to contribute unfulfilled.

As boards take charge of how they work, they must also take charge of what they work on. They must be vigilant to focus their limited time and attention on the issues that are most important to the company's success. Every board has to contend with compliance issues and administrative details, but they can't afford to get bogged down in them. Compliance is a necessity, but it doesn't make a board a competitive advantage. To fully evolve and contribute, boards must meet the challenge of keeping one eye on compliance and a second eye on the issues that are central to the business.

One way to ensure that the board is talking about the things that really matter is to consider the *Ten Questions Every Director Should Ask*. This is a set of questions to which directors should, but often don't, know the answers. The questions are a way to test whether directors are really on top of the things that could make or break the company. They are formulated to get directors thinking about issues that constitute the real work of the board and to identify gaps in their understanding of the business.

There's a lot to talk about. A second way to make sure directors are using their time and energy to full advantage is to use a *Twelve-Month Agenda*. It forces boards and the CEO to agree on and prioritize the most critical topics. It guarantees that those topics don't get short shrift over the course of the coming year.

The Ten Questions and the Twelve-Month Agenda focus the board's time and attention on what directors will recognize to be the real work of the board.

The Ten Questions Every Director Should Ask

Asking the right questions is at the very heart of good corporate governance. Incisive questions unearth important insights that need to be brought to light and explored further—the key assumptions on which growth is predicated, the early warning signs of a liquidity crunch, or the most promising up-and-coming leaders, for example. Thus knowing what questions to ask is of paramount importance.

The Ten Questions is a tool that directors can use to identify where further dialogue should be directed. The purpose of the questions is to help the directors discover for themselves the areas on which the board might wish to spend more time. In many cases, a question opens the door to more questions. In fact, each of the Ten Questions leads to a set of follow-ups that determine how well-rounded an individual's—and a board's—knowledge is of the issue.

Question 1: Do you have the right CEO?

This question alone goes a long way in making the board a competitive advantage. The single most important thing you can do as a director is be at peace with yourself on this question. Further, if you are comfortable that this is the right CEO, how are you going to help this valuable officer get better? If you are not comfortable with the CEO, what are the board's plans to do something about it?

Beyond the current CEO, a director must also be comfortable with the succession process. Does the board own it? How disciplined is it—in the case of either an emergency or a planned retirement? How well do you know internal candidates? If you're not satisfied with the internal candidates, what is your plan to recruit from the outside? How rigorous is your selection process? These are the questions that should keep directors up at night.

Question 2: How well is the CEO's compensation linked to actual performance?

The CEO's compensation is a critical link between the board's philosophy for the company and the actions the CEO will take. Because the CEO's job is so multifaceted, no single measure of performance could possibly reflect what the board has in mind, which means the board can't sit back and simply say, "We pay the CEO to boost the stock price." Directors must be clear on how compensation reflects both the board's philosophy and the company's actual performance. Is performance measurement clear? Will the compensation plan encourage the right behaviors?

Of course, the final compensation number is the one that will ultimately appear in the headlines. With that in mind, have you done the math to see how much all the components of compensation could total? If the CEO retires early, what's the total value? With regard to equity compensation, have you considered scenarios of sharp market movements? The compensation plan must remain fundamentally relevant under these circumstances. If the stock price rises to $150, for instance, how much does the CEO stand to make? What if it falls to $10?

Question 3: Do you have a precise understanding of the money-making recipe in the chosen strategy?

No two companies have exactly the same recipe for making money, not even competitors in the same segments. Some may appear to be similar, but all businesses, whether corner grocers or Fortune 500 companies, have different and unique approaches. Directors have to understand a company's strategy and how it translates into a money-making recipe. Understanding how a company, a division, or a major product category makes money is crucial. What makes it distinct from competitors and how long will the competitive advantage last? Will investors value the strategy the way it is intended? Do fellow directors have the same understanding of strategy and money making?

As the answer to this question emerges, it will reveal the key assumptions on which the strategy and money making hinge—garnering more shelf space at Wal-Mart, for example, or improving the returns on R&D investments. Relevant activities can then be incorporated in CEO evaluation, compensation, and performance monitoring.

Question 4: Is the management team looking at external trends and diagnosing the opportunities and threats presented?

The prosperity and survival of the corporation is dependent on adjusting to changes in the external environment. These changes come from a variety of sources: competition from within the industry, new entrants, technology changes, new distribution channels, regulation and legislation, activists, global economic trends, and so on. A company's strategy only makes sense within this current and future context. So a board must be satisfied that management has properly assessed external trends, has a plan to address both the emerging opportunities and looming threats, and continues to be exceptionally alert to changes. Are rival firms getting in or out of one of your key businesses? Is the competitive dynamic within the industry changing? Are there drivers of change in market segmentation? How well are you, as a director, contributing to the detection of these patterns?

Question 5: What are the sources of organic growth?

All public companies have to grow. Though acquisitions play a role, companies with longevity have always used organic growth to create long-term shareholder value. Is the CEO's growth plan grounded in reality, not wishful thinking? Has management gone over the plan with the board and kept the board up-to-date on progress? Is organic growth factored into the compensation package of the CEO and other leaders? Is it good growth—that is, growth that is sustainable, profitable, and capital efficient?

In some businesses and industries, growth emerges from extensive investment in long-term capital projects. Think pharmaceuticals or semiconductors. Are you periodically informed as to how those projects are progressing, which ones still show promise, which ones are fizzling out, and how much capital is being invested in these projects? In other businesses and industries, growth might depend on the latest wave of product introductions or on geographic expansion. Are you monitoring the markets on which the company's growth is predicated?

Question 6: How rigorous is the process for developing the leadership gene pool?

A critical success factor for the long term is the quality of the company's human resources. The success of the company is directly linked to the right leadership and skill mix at all levels of the corporation. With a superior leadership gene pool, a company will survive short-term bumps in the road and come out ahead in the long term. How comfortable are you with the set of filters through which leaders are selected, promoted, and developed? How often does the board review it? Has management identified trends that will affect the company's future needs? How is management refreshing the leadership gene pool against those needs at all levels? Is the desire to maximize short-term financial success suppressing the continuous development of the leadership gene pool? What major investments or initiatives are being made?

Question 7: Do you have the right approach to diagnosing financial health?

When the most savvy directors (and investors, too, for that matter), people like the legendary Warren Buffett, assess a company, they look at cash flow first, not net income or earnings. Tracking cash is the best way to see how the various parts of the business work together. The idea is to use cash flow to quickly reveal which business units are performing and which aren't, and to detect changes in the pattern. Where is cash coming from? Where is cash going? How do the inflows and outflows work together to create value?

Just as important, directors must be comfortable that the company will survive should adverse circumstances arise. Boards need to keep an eye on the company's long-term obligations, including its pension funding and off-balance-sheet financing. Let a debt burden get too big, and a major problem looms if business doesn't work out according to plan. High debt reduces management's margin for error; it can hamstring efforts to grow and can magnify risks.

Question 8: Are you examining measures that capture the root causes of performance?

For most businesses, accounting figures—revenue recognition, costs, inventories, and the like—are a historical aggregation of estimates. They provide little insight into how the business is executing today. Progressive boards identify the physical drivers whose performance today will manifest in accounting figures tomorrow. How well do you understand the premise behind each performance measure you see? How do the measures compare with the competition and in the context of macro factors such as changes in the economy?

Question 9: Do you get bad news from management in time and unvarnished?

Even the best of companies will stumble on occasion. Whether a key microprocessor is producing a calculation error or a flagship product is tainted in one country, the board needs to hear the bad news—promptly. Is management sharing bad news with the board? If not, why not? If so, is management's plan to address the bad news credible? In some cases, board members have provided sage guidance for management, for example, to settle a lawsuit rather than fight it. That can happen only if management shares the bad news.

Question 10: How productive are executive sessions?

Executive sessions are a critical vehicle for directors to air their feelings, test their hypotheses, and reach a group viewpoint on items that really matter. The board can make a CEO more productive—or it can dilute the power of the CEO. Is the board coming to a consensus viewpoint on the handful of most important issues? How accurate and precise is the feedback given to the CEO? How constructive and useful is the feedback? What has been the CEO's response and follow-through?

Turning Questions into Answers

In pondering the Ten Questions, a director who is not completely comfortable with the answers should bring up the issue in executive session. The board might want to raise the importance of the issue on the agenda and increase the depth of dialogue on the topic.

The same questions could then be directed to management. The process of interacting with management over the answers can be illuminating. Discussion on these issues isn't done merely to hear management's answers. Directors should unmask the assumptions behind the answers, and listen to how those answers are delivered. The process need not—and should not—feel like an interrogation; the gotcha approach is unproductive. What is needed is a conversation—an unscripted exchange conducted in plain language.

If that engagement feels stilted, if questions are dismissed or glossed over with platitudes, or if management responds with slick charts and graphs that skirt the tough issues, a director must press on to really understand how the company is performing.

The fact that a director is raising these questions signals to management what the board believes is important. Just asking them is a good way to get the company's top managers focused on the right issues—even if they don't have the right answers just yet.

The Twelve-Month Agenda

When a very accomplished CEO told me of his frustrations over nitpicky operations questions in the boardroom, meeting after meeting, I asked him what he routinely presented to his board. As he stopped to consider his answer, I could see the imaginary light bulb turn on over his head. The first part of the meeting was always occupied with the most recent financial results, which he and a few key people walked through line by line. If his presentation focused on short-term performance and operational details, what did he expect his board to follow with? He got just what you might expect: nitpicky questions.

Directors have the same frustrations over too much discussion of operations, financial results, and compliance. "The CEO has told us there will be a $100 million dollar cost reduction," one director told me. "This is in a $5 billion company with 7 percent return on sales. He doesn't need to tell us about it over and over. He can send us a note and if we have questions, we'll come to him." The board would have preferred to focus on longer-term issues, like understanding strategy and the external context for the business. What are the milestones? What are the key indicators of strategy and execution? This board seldom got the time to discuss those questions.

Lack of focus has an insidious effect on group dynamics. Boards become frustrated because their discussion time is lacking on the central issues on which they believe they should devote their scarce time. Directors feel rushed and leave board meetings knowing they haven't covered the right things. They lose confidence in the board's ability to add any value at all.

It's frustrating for CEOs, too, whether or not they talked about it openly. They think the board is wasting time and micromanaging by focusing on minutiae, and they're never quite sure where the board stands on the really significant issues. The lack of focus creates a disconnect between CEOs and boards and can put a good CEO on edge.

The Twelve-Month Agenda is a tool that keeps the big picture in focus and improves the return on the board's time. I've seen CEOs propose it, and boards snap it up. A Twelve-Month Agenda is an outline of key topics for the upcoming year that reflects input from management and the board. It articulates and prioritizes those topics and ensures that the board blocks out sufficient time for whatever is agreed to be most important. Everything else gets pushed down in the list of priorities.

With a Twelve-Month Agenda in place, the board's time management improves because directors plainly see how much there is to cover. A director may be less likely to ask repeated questions about a stable business unit's performance, for example, knowing that the Twelve-Month Agenda calls for a discussion of how that unit's prospects will change as a result of a competitor's new offering. And management will be prepared to have detailed discussions on emerging technologies or pending legislation. The agenda is inherently forward-looking, getting boards to anticipate trends that lead to long-term performance.

The Twelve-Month Agenda in Practice

A Twelve-Month Agenda is neither a meeting agenda nor a meeting schedule. It lists very specific, forward-looking discussion points that the board and management jointly decide must be addressed at some point in the coming year. How and when those discussions take place will be determined as the board proceeds. One board divides these into five categories to ensure that none of these overarching issues are ignored:

- Compliance
- Operating effectiveness
- Strategy
- People
- Urgent concerns

Categorizing issues this way shows the kinds of issues that are being neglected by, say, letting reviews of 10-Qs and 10-Ks dominate meeting time. Clearing the routine items by sending information ahead of time, managing discussion time, or creating a consent agenda provides more time during board meetings for discussion of the bigger issues, such as shifts in strategy. The board might want to discuss external issues, such as a dramatic increase in oil prices that could affect the structure, competitive dynamic, and profitability of the industry—and possibly the strategy of the company itself—in coming years.

People processes are equally important in the long-term perpetuation of the company. In fact, I believe that succession planning and management development have to be the focus of boardroom discussions at two or more board meetings per year. Directors have to take the time to get to know the leadership gene pool (as described in Chapter Nine) and cross-check their opinions of up-and-coming leaders in the boardroom. Beyond the discussion of individuals, specific agenda items might include the development process of the global leadership pool with appropriate diversity, particularly if a company is expecting an increasing percentage of future earnings to come from non-U.S. markets.

Obviously, urgent concerns will take precedence when they emerge. By including this category, the board can build flexibility into its Twelve-Month Agenda. Takeover bids happen; key employees leave. The board must be able to set time aside for them without losing its focus on the other Twelve-Month Agenda items.

Creating the Twelve-Month Agenda

The key to creating a Twelve-Month Agenda is discipline and prioritization. Deciding what belongs on the Twelve-Month Agenda requires some insight into the business and is best performed with input from both directors and management. The CEO at one firm proposed a list of items to be discussed for 2004, and invited directors to provide their own items. Together, they agreed on a final list of issues for the upcoming year.

Generally, the lead director and the Chair of the Governance Committee (or Nominating Committee) will work with the CEO to draft the Twelve-Month Agenda, ideally in the fall for the year beginning in January. The lead director should take the time to touch base with other directors personally to get a sense for what they feel belongs on the list, and consult the CEO to see what seems important from management's point of view. "Each of us has to work on the agenda," Jeff Immelt told GE directors. "Pick topics that have impact. Anticipate what lies ahead. You have my assurance that we will deliver on the agenda that the board comes up with." The process should bring all directors' concerns out in the open, but not everything gets on the agenda. That determination requires judgment.

The Twelve-Month Agenda does not have to specify the exact timing of each item. Those determinations can be made separately. And it must remain relevant, changing as circumstances warrant and as priorities shift.

Urgent Concerns and Crises

Crises will arise and demand the board's attention. The bursting of the dot-com bubble in 2000, discovery of an accounting irregularity, or the resignation (or demise) of a CEO—any sudden event or misfortune can force an issue onto the agenda. The board and management have to deal with it at once.

It helps, though, if boards think some things through before a crisis erupts. Boards that are on top of the CEO succession process, for example, usually have one or two names in mind, just in case something happens to the CEO. When the CEO of TRW resigned unexpectedly in 2002, his board was caught unaware—and unprepared. There was no internal candidate who could take over. Within three days, the board received a takeover bid from Northrop Grumman, which had been lying in wait. Without a succession plan that could put a credible CEO in place quickly, the board had to capitulate to the takeover.

Contrast that with the speed with which the McDonald's board was able to act after CEO Jim Cantalupo's untimely demise in 2004. The board held a meeting and was able to name president and COO Charlie Bell as its new CEO within hours. Other companies are prepared to name an interim CEO, perhaps a board member, while they prepare a search for a CEO. But even these companies typically have a short list of candidates so they can move quickly.

The board should also watch for how headline issues affect the company. If, for example, a competitor's cost structure is changing because it is outsourcing its back office to India, it could have serious implications for the business. These issues should appear on the agenda as they emerge. It's okay to push other issues to the back burner temporarily in deference to hot issues, as long as the board doesn't get trapped in long-winded discussions of current events.

To be better prepared, some boards take the time to think about what outside specialists—attorneys, accountants, investment bankers, public affairs advisers, and so on—might be needed. Speaking informally with some advisers when times are good can allow the board to move that much faster should a crisis emerge, so as to focus on other substantive issues that much sooner.

Part Three

Contributions That Count

The tools and habits of Progressive boards help boards transcend their legal mandate and get to the fundamentals of the business. Identifying the critical issues and carving out time for them, combined with good board dynamics and the efficient use of information, allows boards to add value to the company. This is the joy of work for committed directors and a huge benefit to all the corporation's stakeholders.

The board's proper participation can make a huge, positive difference in five areas. The following chapters present best practices in each of these areas:

- The right CEO and succession
- CEO compensation
- The right strategy
- The leadership gene pool
- Monitoring health, performance, and risk

These areas are listed in order of importance. Many directors will concur that Liberated boards tend to invest their precious time in reverse order—more time on compliance and monitoring day-to-day or quarterly operating performance, and less time on the rest. Progressive boards allocate time according to priority.

Chapter Six

The Right CEO and Succession

Early in 2003, a respected director made headlines by stepping down from the board of a Fortune 50 company. He didn't leave because he suspected fraud in the company's accounting; he stepped down because the CEO was not forthcoming about succession plans, despite the board's repeated requests for information and discussion. Seeing that the CEO was intent on choosing his own person for the job, this director, a well-regarded, high-performing CEO in his own right, no longer felt comfortable representing shareholders.

The director was convinced that the board, not the CEO, must own the decision and the process for choosing a company's chief executive. Indeed, his own company had an exemplary succession process with full involvement of the board. So he took a stand on a basic principle: It is the board's job—its most important job—to select the company's CEO. The board's greatest opportunity to add value is to ensure that the company has the right CEO at all times. Nothing else compares.

Liberated boards would agree, in concept. Paradoxically, however, directors on Liberated boards don't spend the requisite time and energy on the process. They often don't bring the rigor to the process or the personal judgments to the table that you would expect for their most important task. When the time for succession arrives, the whole board is not involved. Directors delegate too much to the outgoing CEO and rely heavily on executive search firms. That is an error of omission bordering on negligence on the part of the board.

Consequently, some boards have inadvertently destroyed value at their companies by choosing the wrong person to lead the business. Think Al Dunlap. When the new chief executive lacks the necessary skills and experience, the business suffers, sometimes severely. But it takes one to three years for a board to sense the mismatch and come to a consensus on that conclusion. Thus a failure to select the right CEO can put a company at a distinct competitive disadvantage for a long period of time.

Just look at Kmart, which had three consecutive CEO failures over eight years while Wal-Mart left it in the dust. Or Apple Computer, which struggled to maintain its competitive position as three consecutive CEOs failed from 1993 to 1997.

Conversely, choosing the right CEO is a tremendous value-adder. In contrast to Apple Computer's trials and tribulations with CEO selection, think of the IBM board's decision to hire Lou Gerstner in 1993, when everyone was expecting a technology wizard to replace outgoing CEO John Akers. Given IBM's success since then, it's hard to imagine that it was at one time at risk of following Prime Computer, Digital Equipment Corporation, and Wang Computer into obscurity. Who wouldn't agree that the IBM board made a huge contribution to shareholders, employees, and other stakeholders? By naming the right CEO, that board earned its spurs as one that creates value for investors. Since successful CEOs tend to beget successful successors—witness Sam Palmisano—the IBM board set the company on a terrific path for decades through its selection of Gerstner.

Success is never guaranteed, however. Mistakes will be made. But a Progressive board is conscientious about having the right CEO and keeping its succession process continuous. That way, the board is in position to rectify a wrong hiring decision. Procter & Gamble's board shifted course to name A.G. Lafley CEO in 2000, following a short tenure by his predecessor. His subsequent success demonstrates the value of a board's diligence in ensuring the right management and correcting a wrong decision promptly.

The problem is that many boards lack for robust processes to do the job well. The recommendations in this chapter will help boards translate a full engagement with CEO succession into decisions and actions that greatly improve the outcome:

- Defining the selection criteria used to select a leader
- Getting to know insider candidates over time
- Assessing both inside and outside candidates thoroughly
- Supporting a new CEO through the transition period
- Providing ongoing feedback and formal CEO reviews
- Recognizing a faltering CEO and exiting from the situation while minimizing disruption

Defining the Selection Criteria

Selecting the right CEO boils down to finding a true match between the skills required and a candidate's strengths. To do that well, boards must begin by identifying, with great specificity and granularity, the skills required. Many CEO searches are doomed from the start by search criteria that are too broad, too general, or otherwise not very helpful in zeroing in on the candidates that best fit the company's central current and future needs. The usual search starts with a long list of qualifications—a strategist, a tough negotiator, a change agent, decisive, smart, high energy, inspirational, visionary, high integrity—much of which applies to leaders in all walks of life and situations. The boilerplate may serve a purpose, but it doesn't provide a definitive filter.

Every company faces a unique set of challenges at a given point in time. It is up to the board to bring those challenges to the surface, debate them, and sharply define the criteria needed to address them before the CEO search begins. A company that faces a deep cash crunch and has to restructure its balance sheet, for example, might require a CEO who has credibility with providers of capital and the ability to build a superb operating team. A company that has grown rapidly through acquisitions and needs to take a breather to leverage them for competitive purposes might require a CEO who has specific capabilities in assimilating acquisitions and turning them into an organic growth engine.

These specific mission-critical criteria are not always obvious. Defining them requires that the board has a good grasp of the business and its current external and internal realities. It's likely that different directors will have different views. But ultimately, the board must agree on three or four specific skills and abilities that are of utmost importance. These are the ones the board cannot compromise on; they are nonnegotiable.

In 2001, when Bank of America faced a succession decision, the board took the time to identify the bank's specific needs. The search pointed to a very different kind of leader from the long-time incumbent. Sitting CEO Hugh McColl was a superb deal-maker who had used dozens of acquisitions to transform the unknown small Charlotte-based bank NCNB into a regional powerhouse, Nationsbank, then orchestrated the merger with California-based BankAmerica to create Bank of America, the largest consumer bank in the United States.

Through the series of mergers and acquisitions, the bank had established a large footprint in the United States. Next, the bank had to become a high-performance organic growth engine. As one director described it, when discussions about succession got under way, the board began to crystallize its thinking around that one issue: acquisition integration. What they needed, directors concurred, was someone who could bring everything together into a coherent whole and leverage the bank's strong U.S. consumer franchise. Deal-making was not a priority; operating experience and ability to lead the business on a trajectory of long-term value creation was.

The criteria pointed to Ken Lewis, a company veteran and president of the bank's Consumer and Commercial Banking division. He was well suited to the company's needs. He suspended the acquisition spree and concentrated on organic growth, focusing on market segmentation and the cross-selling needed to achieve it. His efforts were successful and the board supported him. It wasn't until late in 2003, with the announcement of the bank's merger with FleetBoston, that the firm was again ready to take on major acquisitions.

Kmart's board might have chosen different CEOs and had better results if it had more sharply defined the nonnegotiable criteria. If the CEO could not master the supply chain, recruit the right merchandising executives, and differentiate the company against its archrival Wal-Mart, there would be little chance of success. Those criteria should have taken precedence over others. The directors looked for candidates with strong leadership skills, a past record of achievement, and restructuring abilities, and made their choice accordingly. They seem to have missed the essential operating skills that the Kmart position required at the time. The toll on shareholder value, brand image, and employee sentiment has been high.

Times change; boards should occasionally revisit the quality of the match between what is required and what the current CEO has, even when a succession is not imminent. They must remain prepared in case of emergency. And they must keep these changing criteria in mind as they track inside leaders as succession candidates.

The Inside Track

Once the correct criteria have been identified, selecting the right CEO requires the board to find a match with a candidate. The challenge is partly in getting the information needed to properly assess candidates. Thus choosing an inside candidate is usually preferable, providing all the criteria match, simply because the board has the time to get to know internal candidates' skills, abilities to grow, and personalities in depth. That knowledge tends to lead to better decisions.

By contrast, consider how a board typically assesses an outside candidate: a handful of directors will each interview the candidate for roughly two hours; the board will be informed on the candidate's past record and accomplishments; an executive search firm will offer its own opinion of the candidate's capabilities; and, in the best-case scenario, directors will personally check the candidate's references. All told, the board will spend four to eight weeks assessing an outside candidate. It's easy to see that a board gets much more information about an internal candidate.

Of course, the internal candidate still has to be a match with the nonnegotiable criteria. The board has to ensure that there is a pool of potential successors who are getting the appropriate development opportunities well in advance of a CEO's planned retirement, and they should be using that long lead time to get to know them well. General Electric's well-documented search for Jack Welch's successor involved a decade's worth of work. As directors observed the up-and-coming leaders, the pool of candidates evolved. Then as the time frame shortened, the list of candidates shrank, until finally Jeff Immelt was selected from among three very strong contenders.

The sitting CEO must help directors learn about the succession pool. During at least two board meetings per year, the CEO should share personal insights about the top dozen or so managers, among whom possible candidates will emerge. Some boards go even deeper: they make it a point to get to know the top twenty to twenty-five managers. (Chapter Nine describes board practices to assess the leadership gene pool at all levels of the company.) Directors will probe on questions such as these: What are the precise talents the candidate brings to the table? Under what conditions would each be most and least likely to flourish and why? How is the CEO continuing to challenge each candidate?

And don't forget: What specifically are the weaknesses of each individual? In the mid-1990s, during one in-depth discussion of senior executives at GE, Welch heaped praise on a star executive. But a director interjected and questioned whether the individual had any weaknesses or made any mistakes. The discussion then turned to individuals who had demonstrated their ability to handle adversity as well as success. The director's question helped keep things in balance.

As a succession decision nears, the list should be winnowed down to the top two to four candidates. Discussions of senior-level leaders should include some context about how the business environment is changing and how the candidates are demonstrating or developing the requisite capabilities to deal with it. Thus the board can continually update its criteria and track who is likely to meet the future requirements and who is falling off the list. If the board suddenly needs to make a move, directors will be up to speed on who the internal candidates are and whether they are fully prepared.

The CEO also should solicit directors' feedback on the individuals. Frequent, open exchange of observations and opinions about people can open a CEO's eyes to a candidate's shortcomings and exceptional strengths, or to new ways to develop and test a person. As seasoned leaders with rich and diverse experiences, directors can sometimes pick up nuances of a person's strengths and abilities that others haven't noticed.

Directors, each and every one of them, must take an active role in assessing the individuals for themselves. By engaging with them during boardroom presentations, directors can gauge the breadth of the candidates' thinking, how they go about solving problems, and the quality of their follow-through. But directors should beware of sound bites—that is, of giving too much weight to highly polished communication skills.

Thus directors also should get comfortable with candidates informally. One board has two or three directors dine with a promising leader the night before a board meeting for just that purpose. They engage the person on what is happening in their part of the business, and how they view the company's strengths and weaknesses. Directors might pose hypothetical scenarios involving changes in the external environment, to get a flavor for how the candidate would go about approaching the business. These what-if questions provoke the individuals to do broader thinking. It gives directors more of a sense for what makes each individual tick. GE directors periodically visit leaders at their workplace. Over time, it gives them a better opportunity to know the leaders of the future.

Another best practice is to have candidates schedule visits to meet with directors individually. Whether the meeting takes place at the director's office or over dinner, the idea is to create a friendly ambiance. In informal one-on-one interactions, questions can be asked that don't come out when others are present. "What would you do if you were CEO?" a director might ask, so as to see the business through the candidate's eyes. The idea is also to gauge how leadership characteristics got etched into the personality of the person, whether through military experience, sports, or personal hardships. It also gives the candidate opportunities to offer observations and judgments—about company culture or competitors' prospects, for example—that might not otherwise come out.

The conversation—and these meetings are conversations, not interrogations—must remain loose and two-way. That lets the candidates learn by hearing what directors have in mind for the business, and both director and candidate will judge whether good chemistry could be built between them.

With these practices, the board and the CEO will over time develop a good sense for which candidates are a good fit under current and potential circumstances. Realistically, if a board can identify three truly great candidates, it's doing well. If succession is not imminent, having multiple inside candidates is ideal to ensure that there is some diversity of skills in the succession pool. By the time succession arrives, there could be a shift in the required criteria, so boards should make sure they have a choice.

If internal candidates are too few or found lacking, the board might suggest that the CEO hire senior managers one or two levels down with one eye on infusing the pool of potential successors. This can also happen through acquisition. At Burlington Northern in the early 1990s, the board pressed CEO Gerald Grinstein for a succession plan. Efforts to recruit two candidates from competitors were unsuccessful. Then, in 1994, the opportunity arose to acquire Santa Fe Pacific, a smaller competitor with a young, highly qualified CEO who could become CEO of the merged firm. Due diligence on the acquisition target included a thorough review of its CEO, Robert Krebs, and his potential to lead the merged business. Similarly, many consider JP Morgan Chase's acquisition of Bank One in 2004 partly a move to bring in Bank One's CEO, Jamie Dimon, as a successor to JP Morgan's CEO, William Harrison.

Burlington Northern's initial succession problem began when two internal candidates were asked to leave because of their destructive conflict, a common concern among boards. Narrowing the field to two or three succession candidates years ahead of time can spark competition among them—which can have negative consequences.

Companies take different tacks to avoid this problem. At Medtronic, for instance, CEO Bill George picked Art Collins as his heir apparent about eight years before George's planned retirement. It gave Collins time to prepare for the job, while the board got a chance to get to know him, and the company could avoid destructive in-fighting.

Will the heir apparent become impatient in the number two position and lobby for the top job, or leave the company? Boards have to think through the timing issues and decide which approach makes sense for them. Because Jack Welch's three succession candidates ran separate businesses located in different locations rather than at headquarters, they were fully focused on leading their separate business units. Internal competition can be more damaging in a functionally organized company, where the business depends on collaboration among the competing candidates. The underlings (and corporate staff) tend to take sides in the competition.

Assessing Candidates

Despite the preference for an internal candidate, boards should not compromise their nonnegotiable criteria to accommodate one. One board wisely held to this principle during its recent CEO selection process. The board's search committee of six outside directors listened to lobbying from colleagues as well as managers in favor of one or the other of two internal candidates. Although the board welcomed the input, it was determined to take charge of succession and go through a thorough review process before making a final decision.

This board's approach to succession was exemplary in two ways: the board took the time to establish specific criteria, and it created a process that deepened directors' insights into what each candidate had to offer. The board's thorough assessment of the candidates and restraint from reaching premature conclusions made it easy to see which one of them best met the requirements of the job.

Here's how it went. The board formed a search committee and produced criteria for an executive search firm to propose outside candidates. Though some directors championed the two insiders, all agreed that broadening the search was a serious responsibility. So the committee reviewed profiles of ten candidates proposed by the search firm, and narrowed the list down to three outside candidates after a lengthy conference call with the recruiter.

The six members of the search committee then set aside a weekend for the sole purpose of interviewing the five candidates, three from outside and two from inside. Committee members broke into two teams of three directors each. Each team interviewed one of the candidates for about an hour and a half. When the teams took a break, they discussed what they heard and what they wanted to probe further. Next, the teams exchanged the candidates. Thus, by the end of the weekend, each team had interviewed all five candidates.

Beginning Saturday night over cocktails, and continuing Sunday afternoon after all the interviews were complete, the two teams got together to cross-check their opinions. Remarkably, the teams had very similar views of the candidates, and a clear consensus emerged. The directors thought one candidate was brilliant and insightful, but they weren't sure he could execute, because his experiences might not be replicable for this industry. Another was essentially an investment banker and had no operating experience. By the end of the weekend, the search committee rejected all five candidates, including the internal candidates some committee members had once so ardently advocated.

In fact, through the dialogue over the five first-round candidates the board began to question whether the initial selection criteria were specific enough. In its initial discussions with the executive search firm, the committee had decided that its new CEO would need to move the business into adjacent segments and turbocharge growth through acquisitions. But through the process of interviewing, and after consulting other directors, the committee realized that there was room to grow within the industry, as long as the new CEO could sharpen the company's focus and culture. This was a pivotal realization in the board's decision to reject one of the outside candidates, whose claim to fame was his experience in substantially broadening the scope of his current company's business.

The search firm went back to work and recommended two more outside candidates. The committee repeated the small-group interview process and decided on a leading candidate. The committee then took their recommendation to the full board, and after two more rounds of interviews and careful reference checking, it offered him the job. With one director coaching the new CEO, the early signs are terrific and the board remains confident that it chose the right person.

Evaluating succession candidates accurately adds a world of value to a corporation and cannot be delegated. Executive search firms are very good at finding talented external candidates with a record of performance and achievement. And boards are increasingly hiring top-tier search firms to let the public know that they are taking succession very seriously. But boards must own the process, clearly defining the criteria, making their own judgments about people, and trusting their own instincts about who is the best match for the job.

Leaders are often assessed based on their success in previous positions. But can a great leader of a single business run a multi-business company? Can a great marketer make the leap to CEO? Can the leader of an amazing turnaround grow a business? Directors have to think through the basis of the person's past success and carefully consider whether it is relevant. Success couched in broad, abstract form does not necessarily translate to another situation and a different set of issues, and a person's flexibility and ability to learn may have limits.

Small-group interviews followed by cross-checking is a great way for directors to get to know candidates, but directors must also personally check references—rigorously. Reference checking should extend beyond the usual palette of accomplishments and touch on areas that define an individual's psychological makeup.

In one case, a board relied heavily on a search firm to find sitting CEOs who could be succession candidates. It also engaged a prominent investment banker to help out and validate the final selection. But when the new CEO struggled for several years and couldn't deal with some very important people issues, one of the directors did a little private digging. It turned out that at the CEO's previous company, many decisions regarding critical people were made not by the CEO but rather in the neighboring office by the Chair, who was the former CEO and son of the company's founder. The board should have known that ahead of time. Directors' personal investment of time in accessing their personal networks for reference checking could have paid dividends if it had uncovered that fact before making the hire.

Emergency Succession

Unfortunately, the succession decision does not always afford the board enough time to go through this interview and reference-checking process. In fact, there are times when the board needs to move within days, if not hours. The board must be prepared to face what is morbidly referred to as the "truck test": What would happen if the CEO got hit by a truck tomorrow?

In some cases, the company might have someone waiting in the wings, as McDonald's had with Charlie Bell ready to go in 2004. Other companies might name a director to be interim CEO while the board initiates a search.

Either way, the Governance Committee—or better, the whole board—must decide who the candidate will be in case of an emergency. This decision can be updated periodically, perhaps every year. But such a practice is no substitute for establishing a clear succession process that begins years in advance of a planned retirement and involves every member of the board.

Supporting the New CEO

Directors have an obligation to help the new CEO succeed. First of all, the change in leadership must be unambiguous. With rare exceptions, the outgoing CEO should leave the board, for practical reasons. Things get particularly sticky when the new CEO wants to undo decisions the predecessor recently made. The incoming CEO should have a clean slate. This is now standard practice among leading corporations such as General Electric and Honeywell.

Board support is crucial early on, when the CEO is unproven. There is a time lag—usually about two years—before results begin to show (apart from character flaws or ethical lapses). Boards need to show some backbone in standing up for their CEOs as they go about doing what they were hired to do. Public pressure can be intense, particularly if the stock price does not immediately improve. A board must be willing to stand up to it.

When Bob Nardelli became CEO, president, and Chair of Home Depot in December 2000, the stock price languished for two years. Shareholders and analysts questioned whether the company could continue to grow revenues, comp sales (year over year sales growth at the same stores), and EPS. But Nardelli and his board were focused on installing processes for accountability and measurement, while at the same time strengthening the balance sheet. They also recognized external trends that offered opportunities to grow the business in adjacent segments and vertical markets. Directors were in synch with their CEO and publicly endorsed his efforts. The board could tell that Nardelli was executing the strategy it hired him for. Three years later, with its house in order, Home Depot was again on a growth trajectory, and long-term shareholders are now benefiting.

Supporting a CEO doesn't mean turning a blind eye to problems. If the succession process is done well, the board will have a full picture of its new hire, including potential weaknesses. Those are the things to which the board should pay particular attention in the early going, and give the CEO feedback on progress on those fronts.

Feedback and Reviews

Ensuring that the company has the right leadership is not simply a matter of choosing the right CEO. No one is perfect. The board can strengthen the leader by providing ongoing feedback and coaching. A formal feedback process serves the important purpose of periodically forcing the board to probe and reach consensus on how the CEO could improve.

Directors should be encouraged to make themselves personally available to the CEO, especially when they have specific expertise to offer. An outside director who is also a sitting CEO elsewhere might be a sounding board on strategy, organization, or people issues, for example. Some boards go so far as to appoint a director, usually a former CEO at a different firm, to be a coach for the new CEO.

At one company, a new CEO proposed his five-year goals to the board and mentioned that he would present those goals to Wall Street. The directors were collectively concerned that the goals were unrealistic. So one highly respected director approached the CEO in his office and advised him to relax them a bit. If the goals are too ambitious, he explained, it could damage your credibility. The CEO took the advice.

The board should also have a formal mechanism for gathering and presenting constructive feedback to the CEO. This feedback process is different from the performance review of a first-line manager in that it is forward-looking and action oriented.

There are different ways of collecting feedback. For example, boards could begin by using the CEO Feedback Instrument in Exhibit 6.1. This instrument, one of several versions in use at real companies, is designed to draw out each individual board member's judgments on the issues that are key to the CEO's and the company's success. The instrument is divided into five sections that correspond with a CEO's areas of responsibility: company performance, leadership of the organization, team building and management succession, leadership of external constituencies, and leadership of the board (if the CEO is also Chair). The idea is to find not only which areas but also which specific issues are in most need of improvement. The lead director or Chair of the Governance Committee can collect and analyze the responses.

Exhibit 6.1. CEO Feedback Instrument.

On a scale of 1 to 6, what is your best judgment about the following?

Company Performance

1. Did the company perform well financially and competitively over the past twelve months?

    1   2   3   4   5   6

    definitely not   definitely yes

2. What are the two or three things the company is doing to support your evaluation?

3. Do you expect the company to perform well in the next twelve months?

    1   2   3   4   5   6

    definitely not   definitely yes

4. Why or why not?

5. Do you expect the company to perform well in the next three years?

    1   2   3   4   5   6

    definitely not   definitely yes

6. Why or why not?

7. Is the company's competitive advantage current?

    1   2   3   4   5   6

    definitely not   definitely yes

Leadership of the Organization

8. Is the strategy robust?

    1   2   3   4   5   6

    definitely not   definitely yes

9. Is the CEO confronting the reality of the external environment?

    1   2   3   4   5   6

    definitely not   definitely yes

Exhibit 6.1. CEO Feedback Instrument, Cont'd.

10. Is the CEO transforming the organization appropriately?

    1   2   3   4   5   6
    definitely not   definitely yes

11. Is the CEO focusing on the right issues?

    1   2   3   4   5   6
    definitely not   definitely yes

12. Does the CEO have an edge in execution?

    1   2   3   4   5   6
    definitely not   definitely yes

13. What one piece of advice would you give the CEO regarding leadership of the organization?

Team Building and Management Succession

14. Does the CEO identify and keep the board updated on potential successors?

    1   2   3   4   5   6
    definitely not   definitely yes

15. Is the CEO's team of high quality?

    1   2   3   4   5   6
    definitely not   definitely yes

16. Do the CEO's direct reports work well as a team?

    1   2   3   4   5   6
    definitely not   definitely yes

17. Is the CEO developing a pipeline of leaders with relevant skills to ensure continuity for the future?

    1   2   3   4   5   6
    definitely not   definitely yes

18. What one piece of advice would you give the CEO regarding team building and management succession?

Leadership of External Constituencies

19. How well does the CEO anticipate real changes in the business environment?

    1   2   3   4   5   6
    not at all   extremely timely

Exhibit 6.1. CEO Feedback Instrument, Cont'd.

---

20. Is the CEO a good leader regarding external constituencies?

    1   2   3   4   5   6

    definitely not   definitely yes

21. What one piece of advice would you give the CEO regarding external constituencies?

Board Leadership (if the CEO is also Chair)

22. Does the Chair involve the board in setting the agenda?

    1   2   3   4   5   6

    definitely not   definitely yes

23. Regarding leadership of the board, is the Chair providing useful information to the board?

    1   2   3   4   5   6

    definitely not   definitely yes

24. Does the Chair help keep the boardroom dialogue focused on the right issues?

    1   2   3   4   5   6

    definitely not   definitely yes

25. Does the Chair help elicit the full range of facts and viewpoints?

    1   2   3   4   5   6

    definitely not   definitely yes

26. Does the Chair help the board reach closure and consensus?

    1   2   3   4   5   6

    definitely not   definitely yes

27. Is the Chair drawing the best out of the board?
    a. in meetings?

    1   2   3   4   5   6

    definitely not   definitely yes

    b. outside meetings?

    1   2   3   4   5   6

    definitely not   definitely yes

28. What one piece of advice would you give the Chair regarding leadership of the board?

The instrument is only a beginning, however. No checklist can collect the nuances of a director's judgment about the CEO. Even with space for open-ended comments, directors' thinking can be pigeonholed by the language of the checklist questions. A skilled interviewer, on the other hand, can surface these nuances and bring out the reasoning behind the directors' responses.

Thus the lead director or the Chair of the Governance Committee should follow up the checklist by interviewing each non-executive director, focusing on three questions: What significant gaps does the director feel are in the CEO's performance so far? What will be required to improve the company over the next three years? What help is needed for the CEO going forward?

For example, Wal-Mart is now the largest retailer in the world. The Wal-Mart board probably has few complaints about execution. But the board does have to make sure the CEO is facing up to the growing number of activists who decry the company's labor practices or who feel the company's size is impeding competition in the nation. The board's dialogue and feedback on those issues could be enormously helpful to Lee Scott, Wal-Mart's CEO.

The idea is to draw out the nuances that a checklist can't cover. Are these issues transient or permanent? What is the view from both sides of the aisle in Washington? Candid responses from a half-dozen or more non-executive directors can yield amazing insights into potential areas of improvement, as well as on the CEO's strengths and accomplishments. The interviewers should distill those insights and bring them up for discussion in executive session. After the board has settled on the one or two most important areas, the lead director or Governance Committee Chair, or both to ensure accuracy, can then discuss the collective feedback with the CEO. As with the feedback given after an executive session, it's preferable to have two directors communicate the feedback together.

What's important is to choose the one or two most important things for the CEO to work on; five pages of feedback is useless. Procedural issues could be packaged and communicated quickly. But the bigger-picture feedback must be brief, constructive, and specific—for example, to identify succession candidates and engage the board for feedback on them, or to build a relationship with an important external constituency. The board of one large financial institution, which in the early 1990s was performing adequately but not spectacularly, foresaw emerging issues coming out of Washington that could affect the firm. Knowing that the CEO was not a political operator, four or five board members advised him to recruit a Vice Chair with expertise in this area. The CEO and the company benefited from the advice.

There must be a solid consensus among board members before any advice is given. And confidentiality and intellectual honesty are paramount. Such an instrument can be quite damaging when the comments become loose talk in CEO circles.

There may come a time when the business cycle turns downward, and the company begins to suffer despite healthy finances. At that point, the board will need to demonstrate the skill and the backbone to make a key decision: back the CEO or make a change. Boards are truly tested under those circumstances, as the boards at technology companies such as Cisco and Sun Microsystems could attest after the technology bubble burst. With a rigorous process to bring the nuances of directors' judgments to the surface, the board will ultimately know whether it supports the CEO or not.

The Faltering CEO

It takes great collective maturity for a board to make the right decision regarding when to support a CEO, when to provide more intensive coaching to keep the CEO on track, and when to ask a CEO to leave. Sometimes directors have a visceral feeling or instinct that the CEO is lacking in some important way. Whether the CEO has lost complete credibility on Wall Street, let a divisive culture permeate the executive ranks, or failed to execute the strategy, there are times when the leader is faltering, and directors have to face the issue.

Because a change in leadership is so disruptive, boards must be certain they are taking the right course of action—or inaction—for the right reasons. Boards should be careful not to act impulsively, but they can't wait so long that the CEO and the company are left twisting in the wind. When red flags go up, whether in the form of missed targets or gut instincts, the board has to proceed swiftly but methodically to get to the root cause of the lack of fit between what is required and what the CEO is providing.

Directors' instincts are not to be ignored, but the board should do some fact finding before reaching conclusions: Is there a disconnect between what the CEO is saying and doing? What is the evidence? Is the CEO confronting reality? What exactly is the CEO missing? Are the CEO's direct reports frustrated? Why? Is Wall Street dissatisfied with company performance? Is what they're saying credible? The board must get to the root cause of any sound bites. The full facts will reinforce or dispel the concern.

If the board discovers problems, there is often an opportunity to tactfully provide feedback to the CEO in a way that can alleviate them. Solutions could be as simple as telling the CEO, "Your work dealing with external constituents in Washington has been great, but it is eating into your time. Have you considered whether you need someone with strong operations skills to work with you?"

There have been several cases over the past decade when a renegade director or two have driven a board to force a CEO to resign. It's infrequent but it happens. It is the full board that must move, carefully, until it reaches consensus. When multiple opinions converge, they are usually right.

Then the focus must be on the transition: What will the succession process be? Who would be a better candidate? Do we need an interim leader? How do we manage it from customer, employee, and investor relations perspectives?

It takes time to fire a CEO and not destroy the company in the process. An orderly transition takes months or even a year from the time the board's red flags go up to when the board is ready to let the CEO go. Take enough time to address the problem properly, though no longer.

When the board has the foundation in place for directors to pool their opinions, get to the relevant facts, and find a consensus, dealing with a faltering CEO is not nearly the problem it would otherwise be. Combined with the careful selection of a successor, it is a tremendous opportunity for boards to exercise their collective judgment and prove their worth.

These events do not happen every day or even every year. On the average, they happen once or twice in a decade. But it is at this juncture that the board makes its full contribution. All other contributions notwithstanding, having the right CEO and the readiness to implement a succession plan when the need arises are the true measure of a board's effectiveness.

| CEO Compensation

Compensation Committees everywhere are feeling the heat of intense public scrutiny. Nothing tarnishes a board (or attracts regulators) like a CEO walking away with a huge pay package while being forced out for nonperformance, or when a bull market makes the dollar amount of compensation obscenely large. Michael Ovitz's $140 million severance package, Jean-Marie Messier's €1 million severance, and Richard Grasso's $187.5 million pay package may be exceptional, but they made headlines and put all boards under fire.

The challenge to Compensation Committees is clear: ensure that compensation plans pass the test of common sense and reward top management for building the intrinsic value of the business. Compensation is the sharpest tool for ensuring that the CEO acts in the best interest of the company and its investors, and boards have to use it effectively. In addition, they need to align the CEO's compensation with that of direct reports, so that the same principles drive the actions of the whole senior management team.

Boards must get a handle on CEO compensation once and for all. Pay for performance has long been the goal, but even well-intentioned boards have had trouble with it in practice. Something goes wrong in defining performance, measuring it, and matching rewards to it, whether it's overrelying on a single measure of performance or creating complex systems that obscure the total package.

A whole new approach to CEO compensation is in order, one in which tax efficiencies don't dominate and performance is measured by more than nominal stock price or any one other variable. Instead, compensation plans should be clear, straightforward, and built around a combination of objectives that reflect the board's careful judgments about what is truly important for the company. Some of those objectives will be qualitative and therefore harder to measure, but this is where boards can shine by consistently exercising keen judgment and business savvy. As Jim Reda, managing director of James F. Reda & Associates and expert on executive compensation, says, "Boards have to get comfortable exercising discretion." Mathematical formulas are no substitute.

Boards must exercise judgment, but they cannot be arbitrary. A compensation framework can provide the structure and rigor to get compensation right and make it fully transparent. Consistent use of the framework will build the board's credibility with various constituencies.

Compensation consultants, HR departments, and Compensation Committees have important roles to play, but the whole board needs to get engaged in the following tasks:

- Define a compensation philosophy that captures the board's intentions for the company.
- Define multiple objectives that reflect the compensation philosophy.
- Match objectives with cash and equity awards.
- Create a compensation framework that shows the total picture of compensation as well as how objectives and rewards are matched.
- Perform meaningful quantitative and qualitative evaluation of CEO performance.
- Address real-world issues like severance pay and getting advice from HR and compensation consultants.

Defining a Compensation Philosophy

Sometimes when a CEO meets the agreed-on targets and compensation is doled out, directors know in their gut that something isn't right. Sure, the CEO got the margin improvements the board asked for, but maybe the cuts in marketing expenditure were too deep. Yes, the CEO met the earnings targets, but there was a tremendous loss of talent this year. In pursuit of the stated objectives, the CEO may have sacrificed something important to the business, whether it's cutting too deeply or subjecting the company to undue risk. The CEO is rewarded, but the company isn't really better off.

Working on the compensation philosophy first before identifying a CEO's performance objectives is a way to prevent that problem. The board should discuss what, in general terms, it wants the CEO to achieve. The philosophy has to capture the essence of what the board has in mind for the business. Most philosophies imply a balance between factors that are attractive to short-term investors and factors that build the corporation for the future. And most indicate what level of risk the board is willing to accept—or not accept.

The nature of the business will influence the time frame. Some businesses are inherently "long-tail" in that the real profitability of contracts signed today might not be evident until years down the road. The board of an insurance company, for example, will probably want to ensure a long-term view of the business, whereas a retailer or trucking company may be more short-term oriented.

Risk, too, depends in part on the nature of the business. An oil exploration or a mining company operating in countries where facilities could be appropriated by foreign governments may have to tolerate a certain amount of political risk. But to avoid compounding the risk inherent in the business, the boards of such companies might insist on superior financial strength.

The company's situation is also an important consideration in the board's philosophy. Is the scenario one of fast growth, turnaround, opportunistic acquisitions, or dressing up to be acquired? A board wouldn't likely focus on cash generation, for example, if the company were in a rapidly growing industry. So industry dynamics and competition are considerations.

Johnson & Johnson's record over the years suggests a philosophy that could be phrased as "steady performance improvement over the long haul, while making very selective transforming moves." On the other hand, a company like WorldCom in the 1990s might have had a philosophy along the lines of "become the largest in the industry as fast as possible." This philosophy may have contributed to some behaviors that were not in the firm's long-term interest. Another company might look to fatten up its income or sales growth or both to prepare to be an acquisition target in a year or two.

The compensation philosophy is the starting point, but thinking the issues through in more detail provides greater assurance that the right behaviors will be rewarded, particularly in four crucial areas of the business:

- *Strategy:* Which is more important, profitability or market share expansion? Different answers imply different approaches to product development, marketing, and operations. Dell is pulling out of the lowest-cost market niches in China because they do not meet the company's targets for profitability.
- *Resource allocation:* Should the CEO allocate the lion's share of resources for short-term gain, or is it also important to allocate enough resources to market development, product development, brand development, or other things that require consistent investment over time?
- *Borrowing:* What is an appropriate debt level? A company that is bulking up in a consolidating industry can tolerate a different debt structure from that of a company that is being run for cash generation. Companies with high business risk, like a concentration of customers or political risk, may want to carry less debt.
- *Critical people:* Are there particular needs on the people side that could make or break the business? A company that plans to aggressively source from China to keep up with its most ardent competitor had better hire executives with procurement and supply chain experience in that country.

Compensation Committees can be of great service to their boards by rolling up their sleeves, sorting out with management what a philosophy might be and how the CEO should behave in these four areas, and then discussing their thinking with fellow directors. Some Compensation Committees have convened off-sites dedicated to developing a compensation philosophy to bring back to the full board.

David Fuente, Chair of the Compensation Committee at Ryder Systems and at Dick's Sporting Goods, and former CEO and Chair of Office Depot, describes Ryder's process in these terms: "Before you bring the philosophy to the full board, you have to take the time to get your Compensation Committee off on its own for a day or two, so they form their own opinion of compensation philosophy and get a clear idea of the compensation programs that already exist. That way, the committee is fully informed and can lead that discussion at a larger board meeting."

At Ryder, Fuente's Compensation Committee did just that. "We basically got the executive vice president of human resources and the CEO to sit down with us and philosophically go through compensation: What role was it going to play? What various compensation programs were in place? Then we could critique them, in essence philosophically discussing where the compensation programs lined up with the strategic direction of the company." Only then was the Compensation Committee fully prepared to go before the full board to develop the framework that links pay with performance.

Multiple Objectives

The thinking behind the compensation philosophy pays off when it comes to setting objectives for which the CEO will be rewarded. Many pay-for-performance schemes fall short because the objectives are too narrow or too far removed from what the board wants the CEO to do. Sometimes they are chosen because they can be conveniently measured.

Many boards make the mistake of putting their trust in a single objective, notably increasing total shareholder return or EPS, as a proxy for a CEO's performance. But using a single objective rarely if ever captures the range of behaviors a board wants to encourage, and it creates room for people to game the system. It is the root of many a reckless acquisition spree that left the CEO richly rewarded and the company strapped with debt because the CEO threw caution to the wind in the single-minded pursuit of accomplishing sequential EPS growth or stock price appreciation.

Using total shareholder return (stock appreciation plus dividends) as a single objective is a problem in itself, especially when it is measured in absolute terms rather than in comparison with a peer group or the S&P 500. Contrary to the belief of some Nobelists in the dismal science of economics, the stock market is an indirect and often inaccurate measure of a company's intrinsic value—the long-term franchise value of the company—at a given point in time. Stock prices are subject to the psychological whims of investors as well as to cyclical swings as valuation methodologies go out of fashion and are reinvented. As one successful hedge fund manager puts it, "The stock market has become a casino without a house."

Indeed, the New Economy bull market demonstrated how large the gap can become between a company's intrinsic value and its market capitalization, much to the chagrin of investors who came late to the dot-com party. In those cases, rewards that linked with stock performance alone had little connection to real corporate performance. In other extreme cases, they predisposed top executives to "make the numbers" or otherwise prop up stock prices by taking actions that, in fact, destroyed intrinsic value. Dennis Donovan, head of HR at Home Depot, notes that relying on stock market values for incentives when the market underrecognizes the company's intrinsic value can be very demotivating to key employees—not what boards want for their managements.

Getting pay for performance right depends on choosing objectives that have a more direct connection with intrinsic value. These could include the number and quality of prospects in the drug pipeline or time-to-market for a pharmaceuticals company, for instance, brand strength for a consumer goods company, or customer satisfaction for an auto company.

To keep behaviors in balance, the CEO needs multiple objectives. They should reflect the board's desired mix of short-term and long-term orientation, and they should not encourage more risk than the board is comfortable with. While there should be a mix of objectives, however, a CEO can't be expected to pull two dozen levers. There are usually fewer than a dozen that capture the essentials.

A quick example shows how this might look in practice. Imagine a hypothetical discount retailer that is trying to regain its footing for the long term. If that's what the board has in mind for the company, the philosophy would say that the company is willing to cede spectacular short-term performance to make sure the company can compete against dominant players, particularly Wal-Mart, and that it will be financially prudent in that pursuit. If it takes too hard a hit in the short term, it risks becoming a takeover target, something the board wants to avoid. Strengthening the company's long-term competitiveness against the giants might mean finding a way to transform the company's stores, but the company must avoid extraordinary increases in debt that would limit management's flexibility in the future. Those are the behaviors that the board would like to see the CEO execute.

From this base, the CEO and the board must agree on the right set of objectives. Short-term objectives might include the following:

1. Improve operating cash flow by x percent over one year.
2. Meet specific margin and comp sales goals.
3. Meet total revenue goals.
4. Don't let debt increase beyond y level.
5. Open z new stores in the coming year.

Not everything can be completed in one year, but progress must be made. A set of longer-term objectives establishes actions that will be partially completed during the year. In this case, they might be:

6. Differentiate the brand against Wal-Mart.
7. Execute relevant systems and logistics actions that will match or exceed Wal-Mart's inventory turns and out-of-stock levels.
8. Improve pool of store managers, regional managers, and merchandise managers.
9. Initiate processes for increasing imports from low-cost producers in China.

The board shouldn't articulate specific initiatives. For instance, the board doesn't have to define exactly how the CEO should differentiate the brand. It could be through developing new store formats. It could be through incorporating high-end design elements in merchandising. It could be through celebrity endorsements. It's up to the CEO to develop that paradigm, which the board will later approve—just as long as it doesn't involve taking on excessive debt, as stated in the fourth objective.

This set of objectives addresses the balance between short term and long term. There are many ways to improve operating cash flow—shuttering a number of stores and drastically reducing the SKUs could generate cash, for example—but not all of them will make the company more competitive in the long run. The long-term objectives are needed as a balance to ensure that the CEO protects the company's ability to compete going forward.

Some objectives are easy to quantify and measure, but others require some translation. Qualitative factors can be assessed on a scale. For long-term objectives, the board could agree on milestones at the beginning of the year and measure progress in terms of percentage of completion. Ease of measurement should not dictate the choice of objectives.

Matching Objectives with Cash and Equity

On the other side of the pay-for-performance equation are the specific components of compensation itself. Compensation plans are most powerful when the time horizons of the awards are matched to the time horizons of the objectives. Cash bonuses are best used as a reward for annual performance objectives. Equity awards, on the other hand, when used with a long vesting period, will encourage a CEO to look out for the long term.

The optimum balance between the two depends on the industry and the external conditions. The baseline could be 50:50. But in a commodity business such as copper mining, 80 percent cash and 20 percent equity might be more appropriate because there's not much room to grow in that industry. In a growth industry such as high-tech, a good pay package might have more equity than cash to allow a higher reward for the higher risk. But letting any one element of compensation grow too large relative to the others could allow the wrong kinds of behavior to creep in. A huge short-term bonus, for example, could sway a CEO to miss some objectives in favor of those with a more immediate or bigger payoff.

Setting the Cash Component

Of the cash component, half might be base salary, with potentially another half a performance bonus. The base salary has to be competitive, and many boards feel their CEO deserves to be at or above the 75th percentile of the peer group. But not everyone can be; that's a mathematical fact. The board needs a sensible way to set the percentile and to determine the correct peer group.

The choice of peer companies is critical. It's not enough to blindly accept the group of peers from the industry. Industry players often vary considerably in size and complexity. In some cases, a better set of peers are companies outside the industry that share characteristics such as size, opportunity, or maturity. Ten years ago, the board of a Baby Bell such as the predecessors to Verizon or SBC would never have considered Comcast or Time Warner in its comparison group. But times change. Ten years from now, the same Baby Bell might no longer consider AT&T in its comparison group. The Compensation Committee should carefully debate the list and discuss it with the full board.

There are decisions to be made about the cash bonus, too. When the tax deductibility of salaries was capped at $1 million in 1993, some boards began to award "guaranteed" bonuses to pay the CEO higher cash compensation. But Progressive boards do not treat bonuses as an entitlement. If they need to pay a salary higher than $1 million, they pay it. The bonus is only awarded based on honest judgments by the board on the CEO's performance against specific objectives. How the bonus is to be awarded must reflect the board's philosophy. At some companies, it is an all-or-nothing proposition, paid only if all the targets are fully achieved. At others, it is awarded on a scale. Some companies use an objective such as EPS growth, as a "toll gate" to be exceeded before bonuses for accomplishing other objectives can come into play.

Recently, there have been too many instances in which the financial performance of a company had to be restated, in some cases (such as Nortel's) more than twice. Bonuses were not recovered from the CEOs. A positive trend is to make bonuses contingent on the accurate portrayal of financial performance. Reda has seen some boards putting their foot down by contractually seeking a repayment when this circumstance occurs. "It's easy to do, and I've seen it done," he says. One board puts the CEO's bonus in escrow for three years.

Setting the Equity Component

Equity awards should have a long-term orientation to avoid punishing or rewarding the CEO for uncontrollable movements in the broader capital market movements; think of large hedge funds moving in and out of a sector. In the judgment of many directors, the equity should vest in no fewer than three years, to create this long-term orientation. In long-tail businesses like insurance, it could be five years or more. A portion could just as easily vest only upon retirement, to serve as a retention mechanism.

The basic premise of equity awards is to instill a sense of ownership in CEOs and align their interest with that of long-term investors. But this concept can go too far. Equity's value is in the long-term potential of appreciation, but there is also risk of a downturn in the industry or broader market. Thus it is dangerous to closely link the vesting or award of equity to the stock price at a given point in time, because capital market dynamics don't always align with changes in the company's intrinsic value.

In using equity-based mechanisms, boards have to think through the what-ifs of the market and the business cycle, on the upside and the downside. If the market booms as it did in the late 1990s, is the CEO rewarded for underperformance? If the market busts as it did in 2000, is the CEO punished because of external factors such as a looming recession? If so, the board could find itself paying a CEO much less for leading under dramatically more challenging conditions. Boards need to discuss how the CEO should be compensated in those scenarios, and be comfortable with the what-ifs of equity awards.

These days, there is much discussion of the form of equity granted to CEOs: stock options, performance share units, restricted shares, and innovations such as premium priced options or caps on options gains. Boards such as those at Microsoft and General Electric have taken steps to distance themselves from stock options for executives altogether. Experimentation with the delivery of equity-based awards is likely to continue, but the ones that work best are likely to incorporate more than one objective and use a long-term orientation.

Take the case of General Electric, which in September 2003 announced changes to its compensation policy for its CEO, Jeff Immelt. The objectives the board set forth reflect its compensation philosophy. Notably, Immelt was granted 250,000 performance share units (PSUs). Half of those units would vest as shares of common stock in five years if GE's operating cash flow increased an average of 10 percent or more per year. The other half of those units would vest in five years if GE's shareholder return outperforms the S&P 500 total return for the period.

GE's board decided that two objectives—operating cash flow increases and five-year stock performance relative to the broader market—provide the proper incentives on which to reward Immelt over the long term. Operating cash flow, of course, is not only a clear and concrete indicator that GE is executing, but also an important element of GE's precious AAA credit rating. In addition, GE's stock was expected to outperform the broader market over five years, a long enough period of time that short-term volatility would smooth out.

There is another element to GE's long-term incentive program, as announced in February 2003. Immelt can earn a maximum of 2.5 times his salary if the company achieves specific goals from 2003 through 2005 for, as its proxy statement reads, "one or more of the following four measurements, all as adjusted by the Committee to remove the effects of unusual events and the effect of pensions on income: average earnings per share growth rate; average revenue growth rate; average return on total capital; and cumulative cash generated."

Every board must work out the details for its own company, and perhaps change the mix over time. GE is a broad-based company; thus the S&P 500 comparison for its PSUs makes sense. Other boards should carefully select their own comparison groups and their own measures of performance that reflect long-term performance.

The Total Compensation Framework

A great way to ensure coherence and see the total picture of compensation is to build a grid that lists categories of objectives in the left-hand column and the components of compensation—cash bonus, deferred compensation, restricted stock with a particular vesting, and so on—across the top. The categories of objectives could include:

- Financial accomplishments for the year
- Upgrading the human resources of the company
- Progress on multiyear strategic building blocks

The boxes of the framework contain the specific objectives. In that way, the framework shows how the objectives link with the specific forms of compensation. Think of the retailer I described earlier. That board defined nine objectives that operationalize its philosophy:

1. Improve operating cash flow by x percent over one year.
2. Meet specific margin and comp sales goals.
3. Meet total revenue goals.
4. Don't let debt increase beyond y level.
5. Open z new stores in the coming year.
6. Differentiate the brand against Wal-Mart.
7. Execute relevant systems and logistics actions that will match or exceed Wal-Mart's inventory turns and out-of-stock levels.
8. Improve pool of store managers, regional managers, and merchandise managers.
9. Initiate processes for increasing imports from low-cost producers in China.

The first five items are shorter-term financial and operating objectives that match well with an annual cash bonus. The last four items have a longer-term orientation. Differentiating the brand against Wal-Mart, for example, is a multiyear strategic building block. It can be broken down into critical tasks and milestones that must be met year by year. This year's milestone might be to make progress in developing new store formats—an assessment the board will have to make qualitatively. Because the task contributes to a longer-term objective, the reward might be similarly long term, namely a portion of equity that vests only after retirement.

To assess the objective to upgrade the pool of store, regional, and merchandise managers (in the category of human resources), the board could look at progress on several initiatives. For example, the Compensation Committee might review the steps the CEO has undertaken in the recruitment and training of store managers. Home Depot in the past three years has considerably strengthened its store management pool by recruiting some 420 officers from the armed forces, creating a dedicated store manager training program, and partnering with the AARP to recruit employees over fifty years old.

Exhibit 7.1 summarizes the framework for this company's CEO compensation. It illustrates not only the balance in the objectives and in the compensation components but also the *linkage* between them. The framework gives a clear, quick picture of the cash and equity components of compensation. It gives the board a base to discuss what might happen to the equity component if the stock market booms (or busts), or whether the deferred salary program might create what one director calls a "Grasso Effect." Compensation deferred over many years can accumulate into a lump-sum payout large enough to inflame public passions.

Reda notes that many boards are moderating their use of miscellaneous forms of compensation, such as supplemental retirement plans, loans, post-retirement health insurance, and the use of company planes. If such forms of compensation are in place, the board must include them in the framework. One board, after reviewing the total compensation package with the CEO, found it could eliminate a few perks, including a country club membership that the CEO said he never used. It's an important discipline, and one that makes boards more comfortable with the notion of transparency. They need to be sensitive to public reaction.

On rare occasions, the board will need to make midcourse corrections to ensure that compensation is in fact promoting the right behaviors. What if the strategy needs to change in response to new opportunities, competitive moves, or a change in the business cycle? Maybe the old incentives are causing the CEO to postpone major moves for fear of missing short-term targets. Keeping the incentives relevant and working has a huge impact on the business. If the board has a robust process and a framework for looking at both pay and performance, adjustments can be made on a forward-looking basis. But boards should avoid adjusting awards that have already been made, for instance by repricing underwater options or accelerating the vesting of shares.

Evaluating Performance

Evaluating the CEO's performance is the final step in cementing the linkage between pay and performance. The Compensation Committee and Governance Committee will have to coordinate their work to sort out the details of the process. The evaluation doesn't necessarily have to be written, but it does have to be rigorous.

When the board has moved beyond mechanical formulas, it has to allow ample time and thought for considering how well the CEO has performed, particularly on the relative and qualitative measures. Boards are comfortable exercising judgment on qualitative factors as long as there is rigor in the process and in the collection of data. "Considering qualitative factors affecting financial results does not necessarily make the process arbitrary," stresses Harvey Golub, retired Chair and CEO of American Express and currently Chair of Campbell Soup and THLee Putnam Ventures, as well as a director of Dow Jones. Compensation decisions made in the past, he concedes, "were too often idiosyncratic. Compensation Committees would say, 'We thought the CEO did a good job so we gave him a package worth x dollars—at the 75th percentile of comparable CEOs.' Executives certainly prefer the linear certainty that if you do x, you get y, preferably with y based on budget. But to my mind, the absence of judgment implied in that approach is just as bad."

Accounting measures are only a small part of the picture. Getting a full picture of whether the earnings were really "earned" usually means looking at them relative to those of competitors and apart from uncontrollable or one-time influences. As Golub says, "Consider how the financial results match up not merely against the budget, but rather how the results compare to what competitors were able to do. That's how a committee can assess the difference the CEO made. If EPS increases 10 percent but the industry went up 12, even though in absolute terms that may be good performance, in relative terms, it's not.

"Then look at the quality of the earnings," explains Golub. "For example, if your company makes its EPS targets, but misses EBITDA because currency exchange rates changed, obviously results are not as good as making EPS without those effects."

Relative measures can be complex in practice. It's not easy to compare when there are fifteen competitors, some of which are part of multibusiness companies, and each uses different accounting methods. Management can help, but boards are likely to want some objective advice. Reda says he has seen a distinct trend in boards hiring their own outside advisers to cut through the details and ensure that the measures are sound.

He even notes an emerging and intriguing practice: to conduct a compensation audit. He has seen a growing number of boards

Exhibit 7.1. Sample CEO Compensation Framework.

Scenario: Discount retailer with low debt.

Philosophy: To make incremental improvements to financial condition, while improving the company's positioning versus major competitors within three years and avoiding the issuance of long-term debt.

Short-term objectives:

1. Improve operating cash flow by x percent over one year.
2. Meet specific margin and comp sales goals.
3. Meet total revenue goals.
4. Don't let debt increase beyond y level.
5. Open z new stores in the coming year.

Longer-term objectives, for which this year's tasks and milestones must be defined:

6. Differentiate the brand against Wal-Mart.
7. Execute relevant systems and logistics actions that will match or exceed Wal-Mart's inventory turns and out-of-stock levels.
8. Improve pool of store managers, regional managers, and merchandise managers.
9. Initiate processes for increasing imports from low-cost producers in China.

Base salary was set at the 50th percentile against ten comparable firms.

	Base Salary (25 percent of potential comp)	Annual Cash Incentive (25 percent of potential comp)	Equity Incentive* (50 percent of potential comp)
Financial & operating accomplishments for the year	N/A	• Improve operating cash flow by x percent • Meet specific margin and comp sales goals • Meet total revenue goals • Don't let debt increase beyond y level • Open z new stores	N/A
Upgrading the human resources of the company	N/A	N/A	• Specific one-year tasks to improve the pool of: - store managers - regional managers - merchandise managers
Multi-year strategic building blocks	N/A	N/A	• Specific one-year tasks to differentiate the brand against Wal-Mart • Specific one-year tasks to match or exceed Wal-Mart's inventory turns and out-of-stock levels • Specific one-year tasks to increase imports from China

The board has to decide what portion of equity is to be vested after retirement.

asking an audit firm to certify the results that the long-term payout is based on.

There are times when the board should consider unforeseen factors beyond the objectives it had earlier defined, and outside management's control. Successfully navigating a crisis, for instance, usually merits reward.

Boards should make transparent not only the value of compensation and perks, but also the criteria used to assess the CEO's performance bonus. If boards are up front about what constitutes performance, the public will see the judgments the board is making. Even if some don't fully agree with the board, the public at large will see the diligence embedded in the process.

Severance Pay

Severance presents a quandary for boards. It is problematic particularly when dealing with executives hired from the outside. In most of these situations, the incoming executive is foregoing compensation; executives from other firms have typically accumulated deferred salary or unvested shares that they give up if they leave. Thus the newcomer insists on being made whole for that loss. It is part of the price a company pays for not ensuring a leadership gene pool.

The payment is largely in the form of a signing bonus, but some of it is deferred. Then when the person leaves, the vesting is accelerated. The board is simply fulfilling its contract, but to the outside world, it looks like a handsome reward for dismal performance.

Disney's Ovitz problem illustrates the public relations danger of lucrative contracts when severance is triggered. Ovitz's fifteen-month tenure earned him the maximum possible value that he could have received from his five-year employment contract. Disney wanted Ovitz as a potential successor, but in order to hire him, the company had to replace the pay package he owned as head of Creative Artists Agency. Unfortunately, when the news came out that Ovitz was being let go and receiving proceeds from the contract in full, shareholders went wild. Lawsuits are still pending at the time of this writing.

Compensation Committees and boards as a whole have to think through the contingencies in such contracts when they make the hire. If it doesn't work out, how much will it cost? Is it worth the risk? Tax efficiencies shouldn't drive decisions. And if necessary, boards should consider putting the money in escrow and defining the conditions under which it can be accessed. Above all, the total package, including the signing bonus, should be transparent to shareholders, so there are no surprises.

Using HR and Compensation Consultants

The kind of compensation design and implementation described here is a radically new approach for some boards and they may need help getting oriented. The first place to turn is the head of human resources, but HR groups need to modify their own mindsets to understand the board's needs. HR executives may have to shift their orientation away from CEO compensation as an entitlement and away from tax issues, and toward the linking of pay to performance. They, too, should understand the components of performance and how they link to the components of compensation. The board must make it clear that HR has to change its own approach.

The second place to turn is compensation consultants. For some period of time, however, there has been an overreliance on compensation consultants to set CEO pay. Too often the consultants were selected and paid by the company and its CEO, not by the board. That's a dangerous situation if the consultant's recommendations are not placed in proper context.

It's the board's job to set the CEO's pay. The board owns this process. It's okay to have a consultant involved, but it's imperative for the board itself to discuss the philosophy and behaviors, define objectives that link to the intrinsic value of the corporation, identify the correct peer groups of companies against which performance should be examined and median salaries compared, and evaluate performance.

Along the way, a consultant's input can be very valuable. Compensation consultants typically have a wealth of knowledge of ways to structure a package within a context of desired short- and long-term goals, and of the tax consequences of various elements of compensation. Tax consequences are subsidiary to the compensation philosophy, but they are a consideration.

Consultants also have databases of current CEO pay that provide important context. After all, in most cases, a CEO's base salary must be competitive to prevent poaching by other companies. But it is up to the board to define the unique problems that face the company, the ones the CEO will be compensated for solving. The board, not the consultant, has the knowledge to define that context.

Most companies use benefits consultants to support the CEO and the HR department. Boards should hire a different firm to advise them and support their own work. In this era when outside observers are scrutinizing independence, both the perception and reality of a potential conflict of interest are important considerations. Thus, the Compensation Committee should use a consultant that is independent of management and that can give the board the support it needs.

Chapter Eight

The Right Strategy

On many boards, directors are frustrated that a basic question about company strategy is not answered to their satisfaction: How will the company grow profitably, with the efficient use of capital, on a sustainable basis? At the same time, many CEOs are frustrated that their boards keep revisiting the question, even after management has gone to great lengths to answer it. Such fundamental disconnects between and among the directors and management inevitably lead to missed opportunities for the board to add value.

Why is strategy such a source of angst? Primarily because of how and when strategy gets discussed. Most boards discuss strategy piecemeal over a series of meetings, often at the tail end of discussions. When longer meetings are devoted to the topic, one-way presentations of the strategy as a finished product usually dominate the meeting time. Then, when discussion ensues with what little time is left, there's no clear train of thought, and seldom any closure.

Contrast that with the process that Progressive boards use not only to get full agreement on the strategy but also to help shape it. The best strategies are born from management's analysis and creativity, coupled with the board's incisive questioning and probing. The board should see the CEO and the top team present the strategy in their own words, then probe it, question it, and offer opinions on it. In-depth interactions with management strengthen the strategy and ensure that it is realistic. As the strategy is reshaped and improved, management and the board reach a common understanding of it. In the end, directors will wholeheartedly support it.

Getting alignment on strategy usually includes the following:

- A common understanding of what strategy is—and isn't.
- A strategy immersion that gets directors thinking more deeply about the business and its context, and creates agreement around a particular strategy.
- A strategy blueprint as a vehicle to get consensus on the company's strategic direction.
- A strategy monitoring process to assess day-to-day performance toward the long-term strategic goals.

What Strategy Is—and Isn't

Directors are eager to be more engaged in company strategy, but it is new territory for many. Unless they have been CEOs or had P&L and balance sheet responsibility, directors may be unaccustomed to considering the wide range of issues a strategy reflects. They have a tendency to focus on their particular areas of expertise—marketing, say, or finance—even though each such topic is only part of what needs consideration. Boards won't make much progress if directors have different notions about exactly what a strategy is, and therefore what they should be talking about when they discuss one. Those differences get resolved through the dialogue in strategy sessions. In its simplest terms, a strategy is the set of choices management makes in answer to questions in five fundamental areas—the building blocks of strategy:

- How is the company positioned in the external context? What is management's view of this context?
- What are the right financial and qualitative performance goals?
- What combination or mix of businesses, market segments, and operating activities will help deliver on the goals and at the same time ensure an enduring competitive advantage? What is distinct about the mix, and how long will that distinction last?
- What approach is the company using that could help change the external context itself or adapt the company to changes in the context?

- What is the match between the requirements of the strategy and the availability of critical people and other resources?
- What operating competencies are required, by when?

The essence of strategy is to describe what direction the business is going in: how the business will be positioned against competitors, why that positioning makes sense given the realities of the marketplace and of the broader external environment, how the business will grow, and what, in general terms, the company will do to deliver on the opportunities it is pursuing. Clarity, specificity, and succinctness in capturing the essence of the strategy are the *sine qua non* of meaningful dialogue about strategy.

Every strategy rests on a thorough view of the external context in which the company competes. That means the entire competitive landscape—the global economy, regulators, markets, suppliers, customers, consumers, competition, and any other external factors that might come into play. The strategy has to be informed by a point of view about where the external context is today—and how it is evolving.

The central piece of strategy is how the business will be positioned given the external context. That is, it must explain what the business is offering customers, how that offering is something customers really want and will pay for, and how it stands apart from other options inside or outside the industry.

For multibusiness companies, the strategy should explain the mix of businesses. What does that particular combination accomplish, and why does it produce more value than the businesses would if run as separate entities? How do the mix and its management compare with that of other multibusiness companies in the capital markets?

Discussions of strategy should focus on how the broad range of considerations fit together and not stall on the details of any one piece. Most companies will document their proposed strategies with voluminous statistical trends, extrapolations, and forecasts by experts. This data is useful, but it can become a time sink. Directors need to continually remind themselves and their peers to keep the discussion at a higher level: What alternatives were considered? Who are the competitors? What is their cost structure? How do they make money differently from us? What is our edge?

How Boards Shape Strategy

Boards need to understand strategy, but it's not their job to create it. They may challenge management's ideas for strategy, but it's not up to them to define alternatives. The board's real value comes by helping management test whether the strategy is grounded in reality. They do that by insisting that management answer fundamental questions. As one successful CEO and director put it, "The value is in raising strategic issues, especially those that are uncomfortable." Then boards can dig even deeper.

One question boards cannot overlook is: How will money be made with this strategy? The board cannot allow strategy to be divorced from the fundamentals of money making. Management can become enthralled with a strategy and swept away by just one financial target at the expense of others—"This merger will make us the largest company in the world," for example—while ignoring the effect on the bottom line or the balance sheet. The board can prevent huge missteps by questioning how, with this strategy, the business will generate sufficient cash to meet its debt commitments and earn more than its cost of capital. If that result is unclear, the strategy may not be viable.

Equally important is: Does the company have the resources, not only financial but also human, to execute the strategy, and are they allocated appropriately? A change in strategy can require an entirely new skill set, or the withdrawal of resources from a business unit or a pet project. Does management have a plan to retrain the sales force from product to solutions selling, for instance, or to hire new people? Is it devoting sufficient resources to the growth areas and pulling the plug on others?

A host of other potentially important questions arise. Has management considered the full range of external factors? Has it made weak assumptions about how certain factors might trend, or failed to imagine how several factors might converge? For example, what might happen if debt is large, if the price of oil remains high, and if competitive dynamics prevent us from passing the increased costs on to customers? One director at a prominent company believes that the board's input on the external environment is among its greatest contributions toward shaping the strategy.

Are key assumptions about the business valid? Will judgments about the value proposition to customers hold up? For example, the AOL–Time Warner merger was based partly on the assumption that bundling content and recycling it through multiple channels would be appealing to customers, thereby spurring higher revenues per dollar spent and generating substantial cash, a premise that was not met.

What is the competitive reaction likely to be? A move into a new market might awaken a sleeping giant. For example, when South African Breweries acquired Miller Brewing, dominant player Anheuser-Busch felt the hit and perked up; SABMiller and Anheuser-Busch are now playing an action-reaction chess game of strategy and tactics.

How will the capital markets value the strategic moves? In late 2000, Coca-Cola CEO Doug Daft proposed the purchase of Quaker Oats for its Gatorade sports drink, but the board opposed the deal, reportedly for financial reasons. Equity investors were likely to react negatively to the valuation. The *Wall Street Journal* quoted Coke director Warren Buffett saying, "Giving up 10.5 percent of the Coca-Cola Company was just too much for what we would get."

Those are the types of questions that both sharpen the board's understanding of strategy and sharpen the strategy itself. When the strategy becomes clear, so do the boundaries and areas of opportunity. An insurance company—and its board—knows whether or not it will move into broader financial services like equipment financing or high-net-worth personal wealth management; a bank—and its board—knows whether or not it will go into subprime loans. When an attractive acquisition comes along, the company and the board know whether to strike or pass it by.

That was precisely the case at GE. Months after an off-site during which the board and management became fully synchronized on GE's strategy and management's view of its external context, important opportunities arose for GE to separately acquire Amersham and Vivendi Universal. Directors were reminded of the external context and the strategy they had gone through in depth; they had already seen the very slides that now served to lay out the rationale for acquisitions. The board approved the decisions quickly and confidently. Several directors remarked that the context and broader strategy discussion allowed them to weigh in on those two defining decisions.

Strategy links to much of the rest of the board's real work. It points to the tactics operating people must execute, and the metrics and compensation structures that measure and reward their progress. And it creates numerous opportunities for the board to add value.

In March 2004, the management team of PSS/World Medical, a $1.3 billion supplier of medical supplies, equipment, and pharmaceuticals, conducted an extended total immersion session to fully explain its strategy to directors and solicit their input. Competing in an industry with large, well-capitalized rivals, explains David Smith, CEO of PSS, it was critical for directors to buy into the long-term direction of the company. "When you are running a company—dealing with competition, legislation, customers, product recalls and labor concerns—the last thing you need to be worried about is whether your directors support your activities and what you're trying to accomplish."

But his desire to get the board involved ran deeper: "I saw them as a great resource, because these directors have done this stuff before. They have also seen mistakes or made mistakes themselves. So I wanted to get that brain trust involved in the process so it could challenge us, it could ask questions, it could put us through a vetting process to improve the content of our plan."

PSS benefited tremendously. "The directors asked a lot of great questions," Smith explains. "And they brought ideas that we hadn't thought about." Several directors have their ear to the ground in Washington, for example, and could tell the mood of the legislature. They pointed out several areas that could become problems in the future, and opened Smith's eyes to the need for a backup plan. New legislation aimed at curbing the export of manufacturing jobs, one director pointed out, might make parts of the strategy obsolete, which the CEO would need to address swiftly.

Smith is convinced that the board's intimate knowledge of the strategy will help the company move quickly in the future. "If I want to make an acquisition, I don't have to explain why I want to make it; it fits right into the strategic plan," he says. "If I make a move on an officer, I don't have to explain why I made the move, because it'll be clear where we're not performing on the strategic plan or where we need a different core competency. So for a lot of the activity for the coming year, all I have to do is refer them back to the strategic plan."

Some boards have begun to urge the CEO to hire a consulting firm to provide an independent evaluation of corporate strategy or the data behind it. There's nothing wrong with using outside expertise, but ultimately the CEO must own the strategy, and the board must be responsible for ensuring that the strategy is sound. Directors have to trust their own instincts and collective judgments. The right approaches and mindset go a long way in giving directors who have not been engaged in the topic the confidence they need to add value in this area. Many a "dumb question" has saved a company.

Strategy Immersion Sessions

To fully grasp the nuances of a strategy, directors need to allocate sufficient time to soak up the relevant information and ideas on the business and its context, formulate their own questions and thoughts, and work with management to deepen their collective understanding of management's proposed strategy. Strategy sessions are designed and facilitated with the sole purpose of allowing the board and management to be totally immersed in the issues and to work them through to conclusion. That conclusion could mean buying into a proposed strategy or agreeing on a set of questions that must be answered.

Many boards' strategy sessions fall short of providing high-quality immersion because of how they are designed and conducted. Opinion is just as fragmented after the session as it was before. What works best is to design a session that is more like a workshop than a stage show, to set aside a block of time—usually a day or two once or twice a year—and to ensure that ample time is reserved for open discussion and informal interactions. The social architecture can make or break the session.

There are many ways to hold a strategy session—a two-day retreat is often necessary for large, complex companies, while a four-hour discussion can work for a smaller company in only one business. Some companies reserve two hours of every other board meeting throughout the year to dissect various components of a company's strategy. This approach, however, generally does not provide the total immersion possible in a longer session.

In the total immersion session, when it comes to content, three elements are essential. First, the board must have a clear understanding of management's view of the external context. That could include changes in the economy, opportunities and threats, key markets in which growth is predicated, technological developments, news of competitors, mergers, or alliances in the industry, or changes in consumer behavior or distribution channels.

Intel's board balked at a proposed acquisition of a telecom equipment maker, as *Fortune* magazine documented, "in large part because no one understood networking or telecom well enough even to know what questions to ask" (August 23, 2004, p. 74). The experience energized that board to expand its discussions of the external context going forward. Management must decide what is relevant, then present the information clearly and concisely, and in a way that reflects the CEO's own insights.

In the summer of 2003, in a total immersion strategy session, GE CEO Jeff Immelt gave directors a clear picture of the company's competitive landscape, including where the opportunities were and what issues were emerging. That discussion was a useful backdrop for key decisions that came up months later.

The second element of an immersion session is the strategy itself. Once the board understands the external context, the CEO and the top team should present their best thinking on the content of strategy. This presentation must be extremely clear and tight so directors can get the gist of it quickly. Management must use straight talk and do all it can to clarify strategy for the board. At one company, the management team had an hour's worth of prepared comments on company strategy but spent about four hours on it as the team fielded questions along the way. Some directors find it useful to dissect another company's strategy in the boardroom, as an exercise not only to better understand strategy in general but also to develop their skills in validating a strategy that is presented to them.

Usually the CEO takes the lead in presenting the strategy, but an alternative practice is emerging. Some chief executives who have been advised by a consulting firm have had the consultants help make the presentation. Generally speaking, that's not a good idea. The board should hear the ideas presented in plain language, and in management's own words.

Not all of management's ideas need to be fully formed. There may be newer initiatives that management is still testing. It's okay to present these during the strategy session, with the proper qualifier. CEO Smith did just that during PSS's strategy off-site: "I told the board, 'here are two initiatives that we need to do more work on before I can tell you what the outcome is going to be, or what I'm willing to commit to over the next three years. . . . In three months, I'm coming back to you with the outcomes of where these two items are.'"

Smith explains: "This is a social setting where it's okay to challenge, it's okay to question, and it's okay to not know the answer." That attitude helped make his company's strategy session a success. As PSS Chair Johnson states, "The right environment is created by the openness of a CEO who is willing to make himself vulnerable."

The third element of a successful strategy immersion session is the time and opportunity for the board to question and probe. Unless the strategy session is designed to encourage directors to react, contemplate, raise questions, and voice their hesitancies, the discussion will not deepen, and the whole session will be superficial and unsatisfying. Two principles must govern: informality and consensus. Everyone—the CEO, direct reports, other managers the CEO has invited to attend, and each and every board member— must feel uninhibited about challenging and responding to each other, but the focus must be on coalescing around a consensus.

Facilitation

The principal tool to get the board and management to immerse in the issues but emerge with a clear, common focus is facilitation. Facilitation of group meetings is always important, but in strategy immersion sessions that importance is magnified. If dialogue slips off course, entire days can be lost. It takes a skilled facilitator to catalyze participation from every director, to make sure directors get answers to their questions, to recognize when consensus is emerging, and to help define the outcome and next steps.

Some CEOs and Chairs are very skilled at facilitation and can infuse the environment with the informality needed for rich dialogue.

Other times, the lead director or another director may want to take the reins. If the process is particularly new, it might make sense to bring in an outside facilitator, someone with whom both the board and management are comfortable, who can ensure the dialogue is robust and the process is rich.

Informality and consensus are further enhanced through the use of breakout groups, an emerging best practice that can be built into any strategy immersion session.

Breakout Groups

"It's a real challenge for a CEO to get a dozen directors on the same page when they meet only six or eight times per year, dealing with a jam-packed agenda," says John Luke, Chair and CEO of MeadWestvaco and a director at The Bank of New York and The Timken Company. So when Luke needs to focus directors on topics like strategy, he employs a practice also being used at GE and DuPont among other boards: breakout groups.

Breakout groups are simple to orchestrate and profoundly useful as a means of reaching consensus on company strategy. The practice is to assign directors and managers to meet in small groups—two directors each with two managers—to discuss the strategy in more depth or to answer preassigned questions.

The value of breakout groups lies in the group dynamics. Small group dynamics are very different from large group dynamics. Small groups tend to have freer, more informal interaction, whereas large groups tend to be more formal. Having directors and managers meet in smaller groups lowers the threshold for directors to voice their thoughts and questions.

PSS set up a breakout discussion period following management's overview of strategy. Two board members and two members of management sat at each table and discussed the same topics. The first topic was simply, What positives do you see in the plan? This not only allowed directors to focus on what they understood to be the positive aspects of the strategy but also gave management the chance to respond and explain further.

Other questions can prompt directors to probe deeper: What are we missing? What questions struck you as you listened to the strategic plan? And, Where is your discomfort?

Some two-day strategy immersion sessions block out the entire afternoon of the first day for small group discussions. Seating directors and managers at small tables in the evening allows informal conversations to continue.

The pairings in breakout groups should be carefully considered ahead of time. Mixing up the combinations of people prevents cliques from forming and gives directors the chance to get to know a wider range of managers.

When the breakout groups reconvene, as they must, participants are often highly energized and focused. That's when the real breakthroughs often occur. The next step is to get the whole board to come to a consensus.

Consensus

When the entire team of directors and managers reassembles, each breakout group should present the highlights of its conversation. The issues are then discussed among the whole group. Sometimes a question comes up that causes management to rethink part of the plan.

At two-day off-sites, directors are often charged up when they meet over breakfast on the second day. After sleeping on what they heard the preceding day, they come together with a heightened comfort level regarding the strategy and the management team. They also come together with nagging questions on specific elements of the strategy. In the end, directors must get those last few questions on the table, garner consensus on strategy, and provide feedback to management as to what assumptions need further testing, and what concerns are outstanding.

Sunday morning of one off-site, management moved quickly through findings and observations from the preceding day and gathered the directors around a single articulation of strategy. The strategy included expanding into an adjacent area for growth. The management team had experimented on a small scale and demonstrated its success. But one director asked a probing question: "What will it take to scale it up, and how will it affect the market dynamics when the company is operating at full scale in this segment?"

They clearly weren't done yet. Another director asked, "What microsegment of the market is the competition likely not to touch?"

The insights generated through the discussion that followed were again very helpful for the management team. Some questions couldn't be answered on the spot but management pledged to get back to the board.

Getting to consensus is as much to make sure everyone is in agreement as it is to make sure the strategy is robust. Does the strategy make sense? Does it require modification? Directors will have different views on the risks and benefits inherent in the strategy. Here, the directors' diverse experiences and specializations are a boon, enabling the group to kick around different ideas and come at the strategy from different angles. When the board discusses them as a group with management, opinion will typically coalesce around a few central ideas. The session must end with full agreement on those ideas and with take-aways and next steps for the board and for management. The board can follow up with shorter discussions in subsequent meetings.

Follow-up activities build on the strategy session. Management and the board together should use what they learned to revisit and rationalize the board's Twelve-Month Agenda. Further, the common understanding of strategy should lead naturally into the definition of key metrics that become part of the information architecture. Having put the strategy through the wringer, directors and management should be able to identify the operational metrics—the leading indicators that signal the company's future performance—as well as the few key metrics that track progress in implementing the strategy.

Committees must likewise follow through on their new understanding of strategy. The Compensation Committee, for example, should reexamine the compensation philosophy to make sure that its objectives are properly linked to the strategy. If the strategy is going in new directions, it could have implications for the Audit Committee as well, in setting controls and reporting standards, for example, with cross-border accounting. Even the composition of the Audit Committee may have to change. One large high-tech company projected that in ten years some 70–80 percent of its business would come from China and India. With that in mind, the board determined as a next step that the Audit Committee should recruit an executive with a background in China.

Strategy Blueprint

Boards and managements reach consensus on strategy through dialogue, but a carefully prepared document can facilitate communication. A *strategy blueprint,* a four- to eight-page document that summarizes in plain language the strategy and its building blocks, is a useful tool for jump-starting strategy discussions and cementing the board-management relationship.

The idea of a strategy blueprint is to give directors information they can review and think about outside the boardroom as part of an ongoing effort to seek consensus on strategy. "It's a very good idea for a CEO to send a strategy blueprint a few pages long to directors—before they discuss the strategy," says Tyco's Krol. "That way the board doesn't get surprised by anything in a strategy immersion."

In preparing a document that can be easily read and understood without verbal explanation, management is forced to be very specific, clear, and concise. And giving directors time to reflect on the ideas helps prevent those so-called knee-jerk reactions. This is an approach several companies have used with great success.

Elements of the blueprint are much the same as what management ideally presents during a strategy session. The blueprint should begin with a succinct review of the external context for the business. Next, the document must identify the building blocks of the strategy. These are, as mentioned earlier, the components of strategy the company must execute to achieve its financial targets over three to five years, or whatever time frame makes sense for that business. The blueprint must capture the essence of the strategy by answering questions in the six fundamental areas: how the business is positioned in the external context, what the performance goals are, what is distinctive about the business, how the business is adapting to the external context, how company resources are allocated, and what operating competencies are in place.

The document also should include the internal and external risk factors that management and the board must keep their eyes on. And finally, it should explain the connection between the specifics of the chosen strategy and the financial targets that express how the business makes money. An example of one company's blueprint appears in Appendix A.

The CEO should distribute the blueprint and seek feedback on it before the board meets. One company's review process worked well and has served as a model for several others. The management team wrote the blueprint and sent it to two directors: the lead director and the Chair of the Governance Committee. The CEO sat down separately with each of them to discuss three simple questions:

- What is missing?
- In specific terms, where do you disagree with this document?
- What additional ideas would you like to suggest that we should evaluate?

He spent two hours with each of the directors, responding to their thoughts and answering their questions until each was fully informed and satisfied about understanding the strategy and was convinced that it was the right way to go.

The document was then revised modestly and sent to the remaining directors, along with the same questions, by e-mail. Two weeks later, all replies had been received by the CEO and the two directors he had worked with, and a half-day board meeting was arranged. The lead director, who now understood the strategy thoroughly, took the role of facilitator and initiated dialogue over those three questions. A spirited exchange followed. The directors had all clearly read the blueprint and put a lot of thought into it. The questions were constructive and very deep.

Initially, the group was far from agreement on the strategy. Many different viewpoints emerged. Some were exploratory. One newer director, for example, introduced an idea to focus on a high-margin segment of the customer base. Over the course of the discussion the board decided to drop it. Other views had been heard before; board members politely reminded one director that they didn't agree with his suggested positioning for an entirely different set of customers.

In the end, the only modification was to switch the priorities of two strategic building blocks. After the rigorous review of the strategy blueprint, the full board had reached the agreement on strategy that had previously eluded them. Follow-up with this company indicates that the strategy continues to have the board's support and has been communicated to company employees and investors; management is energized to execute it.

Strategy Monitor

Strategy has an inherently long-term outlook, but boards have to know how the company is progressing toward that strategy in the short term. What are the milestones this quarter, this year, or even three years down the road?

In 2003, Kodak announced a three-year strategy to accelerate its shift into digital products. It recognized that the long-term ability of the company to compete would depend on embracing the dramatic change in consumer take-up of digital imaging. But how might the board know each quarter or each year whether the company was still on track to make its three-year transition?

Part of the expressed strategy involves an expansion into digital printers. The strategy has been controversial in the eyes of some investors, who believe that market is getting crowded. On the one hand is Hewlett-Packard, with its commanding market share and history of product innovation. On the other hand are low-price drivers like Dell, with high velocity and a low cost structure that is commoditizing the field. Other vendors such as Canon, Lexmark, and Epson have made competition fierce.

Kodak's board needs to identify the strategic metrics that will indicate sufficient performance in printers today to achieve the financial results that the company laid out for 2006. For example, it could ask management to draw upon a third-party research firm to look at:

- What particular position of the printer marketplace has been targeted? For that segment, what has been the product acceptance?
- How appropriate is the distribution? How much attention are dealers giving to the product line?
- What post-sales service are we providing and how does it measure up to the competition?

Over time, questions like these will provide insights into the customer experience, irrespective of quarter-by-quarter financial results. Other research might look into product quality or manufacturing efficiency to make sure the product line is competitive. If the results are negative compared to plan, the board has to ask management what it plans to do. If the results are positive, the board should support the strategy, even if financial performance is not yet where it was projected.

Every long-term strategy, even those that include strategic acquisitions or consolidation, has a set of short-term measures that can be used to determine if the strategy is on track. Is integration going as planned? One board has its management suggest in advance the appropriate metrics that will determine how well the process of integration is executed. This takes place before the acquisition is approved. And management follows through by tracking those metrics for the board.

A telecom firm trying to enter and establish the broadband segment of the business might track number of subscribers, revenue per subscriber, churn rate, or competitors' pricing on a quarterly basis. If the company isn't meeting the milestones, the board has to get management to define the root cause, including of course the possibility that the strategy is no longer viable.

Chapter Nine

The Leadership Gene Pool

Companies that succeed over time are gold mines of leadership talent. Leaders at every level meet their commitments, learn in the job, and move on to new challenges and greater levels of responsibility. High performers are rewarded; those who can't succeed make room for others. The whole organization is vibrant and performs at a high level, is adaptable to changing circumstances, and, when it comes time to choose a CEO's successor, has several candidates from which to choose.

Few boards delve into the leadership gene pool below the seniormost level, despite its importance to a company's performance and longevity. That's a mistake. Organizational competence cannot be left to chance. Boards have a duty to ensure that management is developing a leadership gene pool that is relevant, capable, up-to-date, and diverse enough to allow the company to meet a wide range of challenges. A business that appears healthy today can take a nosedive if good leaders throughout the company become demotivated or leave, or if the entire gene pool has the same skills and mindset and cannot adapt to new conditions. Once left to decline, the leadership gene pool takes a long time to rebuild.

The mere fact of having a leadership development program is no guarantee that it's a good one. Companies like GE, AlliedSignal, Emerson Electric, Procter & Gamble, Colgate, Sherwin-Williams, and, in the past, Unilever, Citicorp, Intel, General Foods, Kraft, and Philip Morris, produced leaders who were well prepared to lead their own—and other—companies forward. GE produced leaders who became the CEOs of Stanley Works, 3M, Home Depot, and AlliedSignal; AlliedSignal, in turn, produced leaders who became the CEOs of W.R. Grace, PerkinElmer, and American Standard. Other companies (AT&T, IBM, and Xerox among them) have had formal leadership development programs whose graduates have been less successful. Boards should understand the substantive differences and know how effective their companies' processes really are.

Obviously a board cannot track the progress of every individual in a company that employs tens or hundreds of thousands of people. But there are ways to assess the culture and leadership development processes that shape the gene pool. The board can make a huge impact by focusing on the processes that involve, say, a hundred leaders at different levels of a corporation. Doing that would require more time than boards currently spend on the function, but less than they may fear. Some 10 percent of meeting time, used wisely, can get to the heart of the issue.

By asking questions, making suggestions about the processes, and providing feedback on key individuals, boards not only help improve the company's current and future leadership but also focus the CEO's attention on this crucial topic. Successful leaders like Larry Bossidy say they have spent some 20 percent of their time on people development. Many other leaders don't make such a commitment.

The board can contribute in this area in three specific ways:

- Ensuring that the company is keeping its leadership gene pool relevant to changing conditions
- Getting an overview of the company's leadership gene pool
- Sampling the leadership gene pool

Keeping the Leadership Gene Pool Relevant

When it comes to leadership, there's no need for trade-offs between short-term and long-term development. The right kind of leadership gene pool strengthens the company today and prepares the company for smooth leadership transitions in the future.

Under recent pressure from the media or faced with the sudden removal of the CEO, many boards have begun to think about succession and discovered at the eleventh hour that few insiders have the required mix of skills, personality, and psychological factors to fill the job. In part, that's because the CEO job poses unique and daunting challenges. Even in a diversified company where insiders have had years of experience running autonomous business units, moving from business unit head to CEO is a quantum leap in the complexity of the job. But succession candidates are in unnecessarily short supply because many companies neglected to provide the decades' worth of preparation required to build a robust leadership gene pool.

Focusing only on who could be the next CEO is myopic. The company must cultivate leaders, from the entry level on up, whose skills are relevant to existing, emerging, and future conditions. Given that conditions change more frequently than they once did, the obsolescence of leadership skills is a reality. Boards have to ensure that CEOs devote sufficient time and energy to keeping the leadership gene pool refreshed and contemporary. In part, that means anticipating requirements as the business changes course or as the external world changes.

Directors should help management stay vigilant about leadership issues associated with major company decisions. Many companies currently face leadership challenges related to growth. One particular company is struggling to meet its projections to increase revenues in China by 50 percent, because it has a dearth of leaders who are comfortable working in that market.

Boards do a valuable service by keeping the important question front and center: Does the gene pool have what it takes to deliver on management's plans? EMC had to replace some high-level, highly talented leaders when it shifted strategies in pursuit of growth. Faced with abrupt changes in a fiercely competitive arena after the tech meltdown, the company went from selling cutting-edge proprietary data storage software that customers loved to selling a combination of hardware, software, and services to solve customers' data storage problems. The solutions selling strategy required a very different mix of skills and a different mindset not only among the sales force but also among the leadership.

Even changes in organizational structure raise questions about the leadership gene pool. In some companies, the move is to go from organizing around a single product line to units that sell multiple product lines across multiple geographies. Such changes affect reporting relationships and therefore the leadership skills needed to make the system work. Shifting from functional reporting relationships to a matrix structure, for example, requires leaders who are especially good at collaboration, conflict resolution, and exercising power without hierarchical authority. Do the current leaders have those competencies, or is an intensive training program required to expand their skills? How will those skills be evaluated? Putting leaders who lack those skills in critical positions can paralyze the organization.

External changes also make different demands on the leadership gene pool. AT&T after deregulation required very different leaders than it did as a monopoly. As the competitive dynamics change for Microsoft, will it too find it has a mismatch between the skills of leaders who flourished under monopoly-like conditions and the skills needed to fend off competitive challenges?

Boards have to prod management to think far ahead and anticipate as best they can the skills that will be needed five, ten, or even twenty years from now. Given the likelihood of increasingly globalized competition, for instance, management should hire leaders in the early stages of their careers with that premise in mind, and cultivate leaders who can work in multiple cultures. If a new branch of science or technology is emerging—genetic engineering or nanotechnology—maybe the company should begin recruiting leaders who know something about it, or know how to recruit technical talent.

Preserving Flexibility

No one has a crystal ball, so a safeguard for keeping the leadership pool prepared for all sorts of contingencies is to ensure that it is diverse, not just by gender and ethnicity but also in terms of skills, attitudes, and aptitudes.

Sometimes the search for talent goes in waves, as companies recruit and promote leaders with the same narrow set of skills—cost cutting or financial skills, for instance, or knowledge of a particular technology. Then when the company must change direction, the whole gene pool is obsolete. That's when formerly vibrant companies go stale.

Boards can help prevent that problem by questioning whether the criteria for selecting and promoting leaders are truly diverse. The Colgates, GEs, and AlliedSignals of the world endure because their gene pools are adaptable. A diverse leadership pool means a broader mix of people prepared to step in if and when their particular strengths are needed.

Companies that miss this concept can become victims of their own success. Take a company like Emerson Electric, which for more than two decades succeeded largely because its gene pool was expert in cost cutting and productivity. Those skills were essential for making the company competitive on the basis of cost. Around 1998, however, the company began running out of steam and started searching for top-line growth. The problem was that its leadership was by then homogenous and lacked the marketing skills needed to differentiate the company's offerings and convert consumer insights into value propositions.

Another way to prevent the gene pool from becoming too insular and inflexible is to recruit outsiders into the leadership ranks at every level of the organization except the very top. Yet another technique is to ensure that leaders stay no more than ten years in the same job—and less in fast-changing industries.

An Overview of the Leadership Gene Pool

Boards can learn how the company is developing its leadership gene pool by explicitly discussing the topic twice a year. A core group—perhaps the CEO, head of HR, and Chair of the Compensation Committee—can prepare a succinct summary of the company's processes for identifying, developing, promoting, and rewarding leaders throughout the organization. A brief overview allows directors to be informed and contribute, as usual, by sharing their experiences and asking incisive questions. The purpose of the overview is to test whether the company's leadership gene pool is in tune with the strategic requirements of the company, to identify gaps, and to gauge the overall quality of leadership throughout the company.

The overview should explain how the company identifies potential leaders starting at the lowest organizational level. What are the criteria? What are the skills, attitudes, and aptitudes the company looks for? What are the sources for recruitment? Through discussion, it may become clear that everyone who is identified as a leader has the same particular skill or educational credential. Or it may be that the filters are biased toward personality traits—things like confidence, intelligence, or high energy—at the expense of clearly defined business skills. The opposite may be true: individual high-performers may be identified as leaders, even though they lack the essential personal qualities to motivate and direct others.

Next the board should learn about development programs, job rotations, and performance feedback processes. Are job rotations customized to build and test individuals' strengths, or are they generic ticket-punching exercises? To add more rigor to the promotion process, one company routinely benchmarks its people against outside candidates. Every time a leadership position is to be filled, it puts together a slate of three or four internal leaders and at least two outsiders.

Directors have lots of opportunities to share best practices they've used or seen elsewhere. Maybe people should be moved laterally so they see the business from multiple perspectives. That kind of broadening may not show results right away, but might prepare the individual for bigger, more complex jobs later, and, just as important, test the individual's potential to continue to grow. GE's pattern of rotating high-potential leaders through various business units serves the multiple purposes of testing the individuals, broadening their scope, and bringing fresh energy and ideas to the businesses.

Sometimes people are promoted too soon, before their actions and decisions have borne fruit, or based largely on time spent in a job rather than performance. Leaders should stay in a job for about four or five years to really master it and for others to fully evaluate how well they did. And the evaluations must be substantive to judge whether the promotion decision was a good one and whether the individual grew as a result of it. Before promoting one leader to his next position, a company hired a consultant to interview several people around him, past and present bosses, junior colleagues and outsiders, to pinpoint what kinds of shifts the person had made in his thinking, and whether he had really learned from his current situation. If he didn't have the ability to learn from each new experience, maybe the next job should go to someone with greater potential.

A company that is producing a great leadership gene pool has another problem to worry about: retention. An overview of the leadership pipeline should include what management is doing to keep its high-performers. Companies can't expect to retain 100 percent of their leaders, particularly those who are equipped to be CEO but might not get the opportunity because of circumstances. Still, for any company that invests in its people, retaining talent is an issue.

The board can help management spot two major sources for leaks in the leadership gene pool: undifferentiated compensation and roadblocks. Many companies live with reward systems that treat people pretty much the same. Whether or not the system is designed that way, in practice the high-performers get salary increases just a percentage point or two above those of people who merely serve time. People with talent and drive are seldom satisfied with that situation indefinitely. Boards can ask how much differentiation there is in the administration of rewards, by design and in practice. If bosses are taking the path of least resistance by doling out rewards equally, maybe senior management has to change the system or get involved in other ways.

Even leaders who are well compensated leave a company if they don't have the opportunity to grow and learn. Rising stars need chances to take on more or different responsibilities, but if people in the positions above them have plateaued, the up-and-comers can't progress. Management has to unblock the pathways by moving people around to give the next generation of high-potentials a chance to progress. The board can raise awareness of this problem.

Another essential element of a leadership gene pool overview is the CEO's review of the top team and of the next twenty-five or so executives, their strengths and weaknesses, and what is being done to develop them. Not all of these people will be on the board's radar as succession candidates, but they all require special attention. The board might occasionally talk to the CEO about direct reports with no other insiders present. Aside from the CEO, these are the people whom the board knows best, and directors often have unexpressed opinions of them. Bringing those opinions to the surface and testing their validity as a group is an enormous help to a CEO. Chief executives trust and rely on their top team, but sometimes that trust goes too far, and the CEO develops a blind spot. The board can help the CEO see a shortcoming—or a hidden talent that would be better used in some other position.

The board should also get information on people below the CEO's direct reports. Summary information presented over time, combined with personal interactions with these leaders, gives directors a good sense of who the up-and-coming leaders are and builds the foundation for a smooth succession process.

"What I've tried to do," says Larry Weinbach, Chair, president, and CEO of Unisys, "is ensure that we talk to the board about the top twelve to fifteen people each year. They've previously met these individuals through presentations or at dinners. Directors give feedback based on what they hear from HR and myself, as well as on their own views. As time goes on, they get to know the individuals better. The first year, it was a one-way street. Today, I could bring up twenty names and they'd have an opinion about each of them."

Sampling the Leadership Gene Pool

Directors are not expected to know every leader in the company, but they can evaluate the gene pool nonetheless by sampling it. They should become very familiar with the individuals in the CEO succession pool and with all the high-level functional executives and CEO direct reports, and they should be somewhat familiar with leaders below the CEO's direct reports who might someday fill those spots. Beyond that, the board should divide the task to sample leaders all the way down to the entry level.

To really get to know leaders at higher levels, boards need to interact with them in a variety of settings. Promising leaders should be invited to board meetings, and directors should observe them carefully. It gives directors a chance to see how they think and relate to each other and the CEO, and it is a learning experience for the leaders. Are they yes-men for the CEO? Do they add value through their own insights? Is it hard for them to see things from a different perspective or are they adaptive?

One CEO was keenly aware of the opportunity for learning when he asked a young vice president to make a board presentation on a joint venture he had been exploring. The CEO wasn't seeking approval yet—negotiations were at a very early stage—but he wanted to make the board aware of the venture, which had the potential to open up a large window of growth for the company.

When the VP strode into the boardroom, he was palpably nervous. He had met a couple of directors over dinner once before and sat in on a board meeting or two, but he had never presented before. This project was his baby, and he was putting it on the line.

His presentation was crisp and concise, and in thirty minutes, the board grasped what he was trying to do. They basically supported it, but asked penetrating questions that revealed several issues he needed to think through: "What is the joint venture's management structure likely to be? What will be the ratio of ownership control and why?" "We're adding a lot of value to the endeavor. If we decide to buy it back after five years, would we essentially pay for the value that we created?" "What if our partner's CEO steps down after the agreement is struck?"

The CEO didn't jump in to respond; he let the VP field the questions and concerns, and learn from them. The discussion helped the VP tighten the logic and see the deal from different angles, better preparing him for the negotiating table. Meanwhile, the board walked away with a wealth of information—about the pending joint venture, of course, but also about the VP. The board learned even more about him when the VP got back to them, as promised, with a full-fledged proposal.

Directors should sample the gene pool outside the boardroom, as well. Bob Weissman says that at Pitney Bowes, where he is a director, direct conversations between board members and the CEO's direct reports are encouraged. "In the majority of meetings I attend," says Weissman, "management has set up a breakfast or a luncheon for me with one of the senior executives. It's a one-on-one meeting, and we talk about the area of responsibility for that individual, what's happening in that area, and what the issues are."

Leadership jobs get tougher at higher organizational levels, and the attrition rate is high. Looking at levels below the top tier helps the board bring potential problems to management's attention. One director described a situation in which the CEO was two years into his job, and about five years from his expected retirement, when he and the board together decided they were "uncomfortable with the breadth of choices that we have within the company." They didn't want to wait until the end of that five-year period to bring in a CEO. "We wanted to have three or four choices," the director explained. "For that to happen, people have to be put in place now so they can be tested and measured." They put together a succession planning subcommittee, which has been meeting monthly to work through the tough issues of putting it all into place.

The deeper directors probe, the better they can gauge the depth of the leadership pool. Visits to business units, stores, or factories are great opportunities to observe leaders at every level. Then, by sharing their impressions, directors get a sense of whether the selection and development processes are working and whether the overall quality of leadership is improving or deteriorating, and whether it is in tune with the outside world.

Sometimes directors pick up clues about the culture, whether it is laissez-faire, entrepreneurial, cost-driven, aggressive, lethargic, or bureaucratic. Home Depot's entrepreneurial culture was a source of pride and the basis of past success but eventually constrained its growth. 3M was laissez-faire, a culture conducive to its legendary ability to innovate but one that allowed innovation to fall out of step with the marketplace. In both those cases, new CEOs Bob Nardelli and Jim McNerney picked up on and corrected shortcomings in the culture. But boards can easily detect through sampling when the culture is geared too far one way or another.

Existing leaders shape the culture, but the culture also shapes emerging leaders. If it is completely out of sync with external requirements, the board may want to ask management to propose some remedies, or it may suggest an infusion of leaders from outside. While choosing the right CEO is the board's most important job, leadership at every level matters.

Chapter Ten

Monitoring Health, Performance, and Risk

How a board goes about its monitoring function has a big impact on the business. The board's approach to monitoring sends important signals to management. If the board solely ensures regulatory and legal compliance and digs into minutiae, management tends to focus on details and reporting requirements. If, on the other hand, the board broadens its monitoring role to include an assessment of the drivers of business health, it helps management be more forward looking and focused on critical issues. The board's monitoring can then add significant value.

Along with ensuring compliance, the board should periodically assess whether management is preserving the company's financial health, getting at the root causes of operational problems before they express themselves in financial results, and assessing the full risk profile of the company.

Financial health, operating performance, and risk each require separate attention. A company can show good operating performance while financial health—liquidity or capital structure—is in decline. Dot-com companies, for example, were notorious for delighting their customers with fantastic (or fantasy) products and services while bleeding cash. Similarly, financial health can appear sound when in fact the guts of the business have been severely compromised. And risk can be underestimated, especially when it is assessed piecemeal, rather than in totality.

Properly defined and executed, monitoring is a value-adding activity that taps directors' incisiveness, instincts, and expertise to alert management to problems in the making and threats on the horizon. If something just doesn't feel right—for example, if earnings are on the rise while cash flow is declining—Progressive directors raise questions. Shareholders are counting on directors' perceptions, their ability to put two and two together, to be the frontline defense against a breakdown of financial health or operations, or a *concentration* of risk.

The board must get below the surface in monitoring the following factors:

- Financial health
- Operating performance
- Risk

Monitoring Financial Health

Financial health boils down to one crucial characteristic: liquidity. There are too many instances of intelligent business leaders losing sight of liquidity in their quest for greater heights—at Conseco, Lucent, AT&T and Vivendi, among other companies.

Boards can make a tremendous contribution by focusing on one key question: Will liquidity be sufficient if conditions sour? Adverse situations will come, whether caused by externalities like a recession or aggressive competition or by internal disappointments such as a failed mega acquisition that was made by incurring very high debt. The board can suggest that management consider what will happen to cash if things don't go as planned, particularly if several factors turn negative simultaneously. It may be difficult to raise additional funds if a crisis arises, which means that operational difficulties can be compounded by financial difficulties such as a credit rating downgrade. What happens, then, if customers see your operational and financial difficulties and become hesitant to do business with you? Bad news can beget bad news, like a line of dominoes falling, with disastrous results. It happened to Lucent at the time the bubble burst.

The same fate befell another company that was profitable, growing, and full of life. When the new CEO arrived at the company, he found a highly skilled workforce that was comfortably resting on its laurels. After years of growth and consistent profits, the company had settled into a strong position in the market. There was no particular reason to do anything different.

But the CEO saw fantastic growth opportunities. The market was growing, and this company, with its sound reputation and deep expertise, could dominate. Contracts were there for the picking. He made a number of organizational changes that prepared and motivated the company to make an aggressive sales push. Revenues began to climb, and with them, the stock price.

New contracts were huge, promising a steady stream of revenues with handsome margins over many years. However, they required significant cash outlay at the outset, so the company borrowed. The profit margins over the life of the contracts were projected to more than cover the borrowing costs.

However, the contracts stipulated an annual repricing of the services; as competition picked up, particularly from very low-cost overseas providers, prevailing market rates declined. Thus revenues and margins began to fall short of expectations. Then there were delays in servicing one or two big contracts, which further slowed the receipt of revenues and put the company in a cash bind. Finally, entire industries' worth of customers were teetering on bankruptcy and unable to meet their commitments; at least two customers did indeed file Chapter 11. Now the company's revenues were far below its projections and cash inflow halted.

The disappearing revenues, combined with a heavy debt load, seriously threatened liquidity. The company needed cash to continue to service the contracts, but it could no longer turn to the capital markets, because the firm's debt service and debt-to-equity were high. Everyone knew the company was in trouble—including investors, who bid the stock down by 70 percent, and potential customers, who feared that the company wouldn't be around to service long-term contracts and turned to competitors.

This company faced a perfect storm of bad news. But the board could have been more alert. The very structure of the contracts—high up-front cash outlays with uncertain revenues to cover the borrowing—suggested that the company could be vulnerable. And the concentration on a small number of very large customers (and industries) meant the company would be inordinately dependent on their health.

Directors probably didn't realize that what looked like a successful growth initiative—rising revenues with projections of higher margins—was in fact putting the company at financial risk. Although some of the negative circumstances might have been hard to predict—the implosion of the two industries in which important customers competed, for instance—others might have come to light by discussing all the relevant what-if questions, such as What if the competition kills our pricing power? or What if we can't deliver on schedule?

Diagnosing Financial Health

The primary tool for boards to assess financial health is operating cash flow. Operating cash flow is like a dye in the artery, capable of revealing problems at the heart of the company. Analyzing the pattern of where cash is coming from (regardless of whether it is recorded on the balance sheet) and where cash is going shows what is happening in the business.

The basic purpose of this diagnostic is to ensure that future cash obligations match with cash generation, stress-tested against various adverse conditions and considering the realism, timing, and pattern of inflows and outflows. For example, meeting a huge cash outflow commitment, let us say three years out, may depend on an inflow from the successful culmination of a huge contract, at which time final payment will be received. That match needs to be thought through. If you are an oil company with high debt and you are almost entirely dependent on one politically explosive geography, what is the right match in cash outflow commitments and cash inflow? Is it realistic?

When boards are evaluating major business units in a diversified company, the operating cash flow diagnostics often reveal which business units are consuming cash, for how long, and which ones are generating cash. How good is this balance? Are there decisions that management is reluctant to face up to?

Financial health is indicated also by the capital structure of the company. What debt-to-equity ratio is robust and appropriate for the kinds of risks and rewards the company anticipates? Often, a decision is made about what kind of rating the company must maintain. For example, in General Electric's case, management will do everything in its power to maintain its AAA credit rating. That incentive is implicit in Jeff Immelt's compensation.

Periodic discussion of the balance sheet can ensure that the appropriate capital structure is adhered to. Attention to the balance sheet ensures that management does not overstretch to make acquisitions that promise fantastic revenue and earnings growth. Some boards have resisted acquisitions that were perfect strategic fits but threatened to ravage the balance sheet. Others have not, and companies like Vivendi have been destroyed by ambitious serial acquisitions.

Boards should do a full analysis of the balance sheet once or twice a year and help management consider its strength under a variety of conditions, such as an earnings slump or a slowing economy. How will the balance sheet look under these circumstances? Should it be restructured now to prepare for the future?

Monitoring Operating Performance

Financial numbers are an expression of how the business performed yesterday. These comparisons with plan or against prior years don't tell the whole story. They do, however, chew up a lot of boardroom time and often spur directors to ask about minutiae.

To monitor performance well, management and the board should first identify the critical activities that drive future financial results and find a way to measure them. The board can then look at what is happening *now* that leads to financial results next quarter, next year, or three years from now. These measures of real-world activities are the leading indicators of tomorrow's financial results, and should become part of the board's information architecture and the subject of boardroom dialogue.

Let's say you are a director of one of the top automakers in the world, examining performance in the very competitive U.S. automobile marketplace. You would probably keep a close eye on market share, an important indicator of how well the company's cars are accepted by consumers, and be satisfied to see the figure improve.

But market share is a reflection of a number of items. Is it because of extraordinary discounting? Or is the customer satisfaction rate improving and thus the value of used cars on the rise? Or has the company figured out a new segment and the new product line is hugely successful? It is these kinds of probing questions that help get to the root causes and allow the board to assess what performance is likely to be in the near future.

Some of this data is quantitative, but some is qualitative. Most needs to be benchmarked against competitors. In all cases, the board has to consider the quality of the data and its sources as well. If a brand ranking is in decline, for example, the board has to know who is performing the ranking, and what its methodology is, before it can determine whether the ranking is relevant for the desired customer segment. Did the sampling overweight regions where the company is traditionally a weak seller? It could be a statistical anomaly.

These measures and assessments need to infuse the information architecture. A good start is to have the CEO or the CFO describe the way management looks at these issues. Then a committee will work with management to design a reporting template to present current bad news and root cause measures—today's real-world activities that are expressed in tomorrow's financial reports—compared to internal historicals and projections, external conditions, and the competition.

The judgment of seasoned business leaders is crucial for getting at the ideas and patterns underlying the numbers. The board adds value not by looking at percentage point differences from one period to another, but rather by having management present patterns of improvement or deterioration, and probing further to unearth what is happening in the business to cause the measures to go one way or the other. If a measure truly is in decline, the board should help management get to the root causes and know what steps management is taking to address them.

Monitoring Risk

In this day and age, most companies are exposed to risks that go beyond financial risks. Thus, risk warrants a separate discussion of its own. Every element of strategy involves investment and risk. Most risks are small enough or low enough in probability that they are manageable. But if the perfect storm arrives, the company could face a threat.

All too often, any discussion of risk beyond financial takes place piecemeal, for the approval of an acquisition or capital expenditure, for example. But it is often a combination of operating risk and financial risk that compound to put survival in question. Board discussion ensures that management has a plan B should a perfect storm occur. Planning for the discussion also influences management's priorities in terms of understanding the full risk profile and planning for the possibilities.

Jose Carrion, a director of Popular Inc., the parent company of Banco Popular de Puerto Rico, points out that the board's risk monitoring job is to make sure that management avoids not only betting the company on overly rosy assumptions but also setting itself up for a convergence of negative factors.

The board can expand its monitoring function by examining the links between risks in the business—whether driven by factors in execution, competition, customers, supply chain, economy, or natural disaster—and financial health. It can also help the CEO stress test the strategy to see what happens to the company's liquidity under a variety of circumstances.

There are many types of risk to consider, beginning with financial risk. How sensitive is the business to interest rate movements? What might put the credit rating at risk? What is the bare minimum performance needed to fund debt service? In the airline business, what is the risk of not hedging oil prices?

Then there is the influence of business risk on financials. What happens to liquidity if demand isn't as strong as expected, if economic conditions turn down, or if union disputes prove disruptive, for example. The list of possibilities is long: outbreak of war, environmentalists begin to picket, an industry that is a key customer base goes sour. These types of risks need to be identified.

Legal risks are one type of risk that boards are already assessing. When legal risks become too large, companies pay a price for capital in the stock and bond markets. Consider what's happened with asbestos and other product liabilities. So boards are asking whether their companies have the cash set aside to survive a major hit, whether a settlement would be expeditious, and whether other legal issues loom. If need be, they hire counsel to advise them of the potential risks.

The same approach can be used in other domains of risk. Any of a host of operational risks could put the company franchise in question, and boards would do well to apply a disciplined process to identify them and understand their influence on financial risk. Many companies learned of these risks the hard way. For example, the bursting of the Internet bubble in 2000 stripped bare the companies that served dot-com customers. Directors should have questioned management over the concentration of customers in any single industry, particularly since few of the companies in that industry were profit-making ventures. Directors at companies serving cyclical industries such as airlines have to ask the same questions. Should the company diversify its customer base? Should it decline a contract that would make the company overly reliant on a single revenue source? The answers lie in weighing the risk to liquidity should events not turn out as planned.

Some suppliers, for example, have not been prepared for the margin pressures and supply chain requirements that come with selling to Wal-Mart. The potential sales are enormous, but suppliers must be prepared to meet Wal-Mart's demands. Many are thriving under those conditions. But others are reconsidering their decisions. They made bet-the-company investments in capacity, some to the point of overextending their financial health. With sales through Wal-Mart dominating their top line, they cannot walk away from the relationship. But their financial health depends precariously on executing for a low-margin customer. Boards and their managements must wrestle up front with whether such growth is worth the risk in their case.

Similar risks can be found in a concentration on a single geographic area for suppliers or customers. For a U.S.-based company, 60 percent of revenues and income from Brazil alone pose a very critical geographical risk, first because of political conditions in Brazil, second because of monetary conditions in Brazil. Many a company's operating performance has been adversely affected by dependence on one country.

Then there is political, legislative, or regulatory risk. What if new tariffs make raw materials more expensive? What if laws are eased to make it easier for new competitors to enter the industry? Lastly, there are risks associated with public opinion across a range of stakeholders. Will we become a more public target as we grow? Will practices attract the attention of environmental or labor activists? Such attention might be grounded in some kernel of truth. Should we consider conducting business in a radically different fashion to head off this risk? These are questions that boards should tackle periodically.

The Risk Committee

Some boards are forming Risk Committees to assure themselves that management understands the major risks the company faces. The committee can work with management to examine the risk factors and identify where risks may concentrate or compound. Further, the team can identify the early warning signals, so management can develop a plan to mitigate these risks.

Carrion describes the process of managing identified risks as fourfold: eliminate the risk, mitigate the risk, accept the risk (and hopefully get paid a premium for it), or transfer the risk. Some risks can be eliminated or mitigated by declining certain contracts or making a strategic shift, such as developing new products to diversify the customer base. Still other risks must simply be accepted. By thinking through contingencies in advance, however, management may be quicker in recognizing that the events are coming to pass, and in responding to the events by putting plan B into action.

While the Risk Committee can take the lead and make recommendations, the whole board should involve itself with risk assessment in one board meeting per year. The full board must understand the most dangerous and likely risks and help management think through the implications.

Part Four

Maintaining Momentum

Throughout this book, the focus has been on how boards can improve the quality of their interactions and make important contributions to their companies' success. The nitty-gritty of how the board should organize itself—number of meetings, selection of directors, committee structure, and the like—is of lesser importance than the practices described in Parts Two and Three. But getting the details wrong or spending too much time on them will surely slow the journey toward becoming Progressive.

Boards also can be pulled off course by external constituencies, namely investors, that want to dictate major changes in the company's direction. All the more reason for boards to accelerate their evolution to give them a firm basis to withstand such pressures.

The following chapters will help boards put the mechanics of board operations behind them and navigate the tricky issue of working with shareholders.

Chapter Eleven

Board Operations

Whether the CEO and Chair roles are separated, how many committees the board has, how many meetings are held each year and for how long—these are the kinds of procedural and architectural variables that many board watchers focus on. Even boards themselves sometimes get sidetracked debating these details. But they can't afford to. These are not the issues that turn a board into a competitive advantage.

Decisions about board operations don't require endless debate. Common sense and group dynamics should be the guide. Will the new slate of directors help the board add value and work well as a group? Does a separate Chair facilitate dialogue? Are directors up to speed in all the areas they need to be? Is the board making efficient use of directors' expertise and time?

A rundown of the following topics can help boards identify the best practices so they can adopt them expediently and move on:

- Board composition
- Separating the CEO and Chair roles
- Continuing education
- Committees
- Meeting logistics

Board Composition

For the board to be a competitive advantage, its composition must be relevant to the times and the needs of the company. The Governance Committee should periodically debate the criteria to make sure the current composition is appropriate, not only when there is turnover on the board but also when a change in strategy or in the external context might argue for new skills.

Lately, boards have been adding accounting expertise. But if a company is shifting from cost cutting to organic growth, for example, it might also consider recruiting directors with marketing experience. If a company is expanding geographically, it might be wise to have a board member with experience doing business in the new region.

There are some constants in terms of requirements. There are criteria that every potential director must fulfill, such as the ability to gel with the CEO and the rest of the board, and the highest ethical integrity. And every board should include at least two directors who are sitting or recently retired CEOs. Successful CEOs are typically the most well-rounded, seasoned, and active directors, ones who not only bring a great deal of relevant experience to the board but also have great instincts about changes in the external environment, strategy, people, and operational effectiveness. They are likely to respect the CEO's authority, and they tend to be good at bringing groups to a consensus.

One board constructed the matrix in Exhibit 11.1 to compile the backgrounds of its non-executive directors, so it could see how the mix of directors and their domain knowledge fit together (the names have been changed). Each row indicates a "major strength" that may be required on a board. Of course, most of the individuals have a broad base of skills, but it was useful to codify them by their most prominent experiences.

Each director had to fulfill the general criteria this board put forth at the top of the chart. But in this case, the board also identified three areas in which it needed to have some depth: CEO of a manufacturing company with strengths in operations, finance, and strategy; financial expertise as defined in the new rules for Audit Committee service; and global experience to provide guidance in expanding markets (the company operates diverse businesses in over a hundred countries). The mix of nine directors achieves all of these goals.

Other companies should consider constructing their own charts, based on their own anticipated needs. The idea is to balance diverse viewpoints and experiences. Diversity in terms of ethnicity and gender is important. But each director should also bring

Exhibit 11.1. Board Candidate Criteria for One Board.

General Criteria

High ethical standards and integrity. Willing to act on and be accountable for board decisions. Ability to provide wise, thoughtful counsel on a range of issues. Have a history of achievements that reflect high standards for themselves and others. Will be loyal and committed to driving the success of the company. Able to take tough positions while being a team player.

Specific Criteria

Major Strength	Williams	Jeter	Rodriguez	Giambi	Sheffield	Posada	Matsui	Clark	Wilson
Business management (CEO or president)	x	x	x	x	—	x	—	—	x
Operations	x	x	x	—	—		x	—	x
Financial literacy	x	x	x	x	x	x	—	x	x
Financial expertise	—	—	—	—	x	x	—	x	x
Marketing	x	—	—	x	—	—	—	—	—
Global experience	x	x	x	—	—	x	x	—	x
Other (R&D, PR, public accounting, government. . .)	—	—	—	—	—	—	x	x	—
Human resources									
Business development/ M&A expertise									
Change management									

specific experiences or expertise that the board will need. The introduction of a younger director can also bring fresh blood to a board—many CEOs appreciate a periodic infusion of talent.

With that said, the need for diverse perspectives should never trump the need for personalities who work well together. The ability of a director to think independently but also move a group forward is the non-negotiable criterion for director candidates.

That's one problem with the SEC's proposal to allow shareholders to nominate directors under certain conditions. It is a controversial provision, which had not been settled as of this writing. While some boards might need to be shaken up, such appointees will be a setback for other boards. A director with an adversarial mindset or a narrow focus could make it harder for the board to gel and act collectively. The result could be a more fractious board that accomplishes less and distracts the CEO from running the business.

Finding and Assessing New Directors

When Sarbanes-Oxley was passed, a common complaint was that it would become harder and harder to find qualified director candidates. Observers noted that individuals would likely sit on fewer boards because of the greater time demands, and some candidates would turn down the opportunity for fear of legal liability. Thus the pool of directors with the necessary depth and breadth of knowledge was about to get much smaller.

These fears were misplaced. By broadening their searches to include direct reports of CEOs, for example, and more aggressively seeking gender, ethnic, and geographic diversity, boards have discovered that the pool of qualified directors is much larger than they first thought.

However, an entirely different problem is emerging. As boards take charge of director nominations, they do not always devote enough time to the recruitment of directors who will make the board stronger and better in every way. They need not only the proper mix of experience and expertise, such as accounting, but also the right skills for group dynamics. Incoming directors must have not only the courage to articulate a dissenting viewpoint but also the humility to know when their viewpoint is not the consensus. Sarbanes-Oxley requires every board to have an accounting expert, which has led more CFOs and accounting professors to join boards. Many have strong personalities and can become a drain on the board. Unless boards explicitly consider a director candidate's ability to work within a group, they run the risk of recruiting directors who could become unwanted.

As disruptive as it is to have one unwanted director, a host of companies find themselves dealing with two or three. One board had a long history of recruiting directors who had either been denied CEO positions or were removed from the CEO job. At any given time over the course of nearly twenty years, the majority of directors were people whose ambitions had been frustrated or unfulfilled. Together, they were a rowdy group that kept consecutive CEOs constantly on the defensive. Eventually, the company went bankrupt.

Impeccable credentials are not the only indication of whether an individual will contribute to the board. Take the case of one CEO who was recruited to the board of a multibillion-dollar company. This individual was the subject of glowing media coverage as a disciplined leader who had brought his company back from the brink.

Almost immediately, he became an unwanted director. By being very articulate, he gained influence on the board. But he nitpicked at issues, particularly at those in his area of expertise, marketing. In consecutive meetings, he opined about how hopeless focus groups are, rather than asking more productive questions, such as, "How are you going about making judgments on consumer receptivity to new products?" The company was in real trouble, but he couldn't focus on the right operational and strategic deficits. And his contributions impeded the rest of the board, and the CEO, from addressing the real problems.

Assessing director candidates requires digging deeper into their backgrounds. Some directors feel they have something to prove. It takes careful and discreet background checking to uncover the true circumstances of a person's career. An executive search firm might propose a few candidates and provide excellent synopses of their accomplishments and skills, but directors should interview the candidates and check references themselves. One board spared itself some trouble by passing over a candidate that

might well have become unwanted; the board's reference checking revealed that the person had had bad relations with a previous
board, and that when that board failed to renominate him, he did
some things unworthy of a director. The second board saw it as a
sign of immaturity.

If directors put their minds together, they will usually know
someone who knows or has worked with the candidate. Phone calls
need to be made, personally. The candidate's personality and tem-
perament must be checked through these references—and directors making the calls should take them very seriously. The questions
might be different for an academic candidate as opposed to a sitting CEO, but the necessity remains. Good press clippings are no
substitute.

The CEO should also interview the candidate, possibly side-by-
side with the lead director. It's a good way to see how the candidate
might interact with the CEO. Will the relationship be combative
or constructive? Is the candidate too reserved? Too opinionated?
It's also a good idea for several other directors to personally interview the candidates and gauge how each person might hurt or help
the group dynamics. The best candidates will welcome a rigorous
interview process, because it will help them decide whether they
can work with the other directors.

Separating the CEO and Chair Positions

As the post-Enron wave of regulation commenced, one particularly
contentious proposal made the rounds: that the CEO should not
simultaneously hold the Chair position. A board led by a non-
executive Chair, the theory goes, would be more willing and able to
challenge a CEO, to truly monitor conduct and performance. Such
boards were felt to be less under the thumb of imperial CEOs.

In practice, of course, this didn't always turn out to be the case.
Enron itself had a separate CEO and Chair before the scandal
struck, as did other fallen stars. And broader evidence from the
United Kingdom runs counter to the theory as well. While the generally accepted U.K. practice swung toward non-executive Chairs
with the Combined Code, anecdotally speaking, scandals and performance failures are still quite evident there. In some cases, the
split position has created a "who's in charge?" soap opera in which

the City interacts with the Chair while employees listen to the chief executive. This drama can be incredibly distracting.

This evidence backs up observation over the years: Separating the CEO and Chair positions simply makes no difference to the effectiveness of a board. The Chair, like any other director, still has to get consensus to be effective—the position doesn't enable someone to enforce independent decisions. The dialogue has to lead to the same place, whether it's a Chair facilitating or a lead director.

In fact, a separate Chair could actually be counterproductive, as some U.K. cases demonstrate. It can create an adversarial relationship and weaken the CEO's ability to get anything done. Sometimes it leads to a board's meddling in operations or dictating strategy. If other directors defer responsibility to a Chair, it actually detracts from getting the full board engaged.

Most CEOs today are already open to the board's involvement. They don't need a powerful individual to counter them; they need the board to find its center. Having an effective lead director who can bring the board to consensus is all that is needed, in the vast majority of cases.

In those companies where the roles of CEO and Chair are already separate, it is doubly important to openly discuss among the full board the responsibilities of the CEO, the Chair, and the other directors. The Chair can be a sounding board for the CEO to explore how the board feels on particular issues. Or the Chair could make sure that conduct and behavior in the boardroom conforms to the rules of engagement. These are similar functions that a lead director might perform.

The Chair should not, however, be a voice to the public. That has to be the CEO's job. If the Chair has too high a profile, it diminishes the CEO's credibility in the eyes of the public and the investment community. Also, other directors must feel an equal obligation to speak up and be engaged with governance, regardless of whether the CEO is Chair or not.

Committees

The number of ongoing committees should be kept to a minimum to reduce redundancies and ensure directors' time is well used. Typically, a board will have three ongoing committees: Governance (or Nominating), Compensation, and Audit. Some boards add others. For example, this book advocates one other committee: a Risk Committee. Other committees might be formed as business requires, for example, an Environmental Committee for a chemical company, and ad hoc committees that form and disband fluidly to address issues as they emerge.

Boards might also consider rotating committee Chairs or even committee membership. If a board chose to enact such a policy, a director would hold a position for only two or three years before rotating out of the role, and possibly out of the committee. It's a smooth way to ensure that directors broaden their experience by being exposed to more areas of the business, and that time commitments are spread out.

Continuing Education

Liberated boards face a new world of corporate governance, and directors should avail themselves of top-notch seminars for directors. This is particularly true for the many first-time directors contributing to corporate governance. But experienced directors should also take part in the programs. The corporate governance environment has changed dramatically since Sarbanes-Oxley and most directors could use a refresher course on one subject or another. Programs hosted by business schools and professional organizations are also great for broadening social networks—useful when it comes to succession and the leadership gene pool.

With new regulations and conventions coming into force, most boards are already aware of the need to broaden their understanding of accounting and finance to improve their oversight of financial health. Top management succession, too, is a popular area; case studies abound of CEO succession processes that worked. And of course, boards need to stay on top of all changes in securities laws, policies, and other compliance rules in the United States and around the world.

But there are other subjects boards must understand, some of which may need to be custom-designed for a particular board:

- *Strategy:* Whole industries change much more quickly than ever before. Strategies become obsolete, business models broken. Before directors dig in, they may want to go through focused education on specific industries, the global regulatory environment, and external trends. They can learn how what is happening in the world affects their industry from diverse sources and points of view.

- *Performance measurements:* New conventions in measuring and reporting performance are emerging, and directors need to learn how performance reporting can be done in a given company and industry.
- *How financial markets function:* The board and the Audit Committee should have an up-to-date view of the role financial reporting and disclosure plays, and of how the financial markets function. How do different types of investors influence the capital markets? How do professional investors make decisions—and how should boards influence those decisions?
- *Risk management:* Boards are taking on greater responsibility in understanding risk. What constitutes financial, business, and geopolitical risk? How will these risks change? What are the ways to eliminate, mitigate, transfer, or otherwise live with these risks?
- *The changing legal responsibilities of directors:* The lawsuit against Disney directors over Michael Ovitz's compensation has set a precedent that could lead to more frequent suits against directors. Attorneys have observed that some courts are taking more active stances on hearing cases regarding director liability. Directors need to be up to speed on the fundamentals: How are laws being interpreted? What laws will be created? What are the gray areas?
- *Top executive compensation:* CEO compensation is a classic area for board education, but it is a top-of-mind issue. Best practices in compensation are ever-changing. Boards need to know what the new issues are and what the best practices are to attract, motivate, and retain their leaders.
- *Technologies:* Intel hosts seminars for directors, taught by the firm's engineers, on key technical issues. The practice should not be limited to high-tech firms, however, as technologies evolve rapidly and can affect the corporation at many fundamental levels.

Meeting Logistics

Holding more meetings won't always improve board dynamics. Holding longer meetings won't ensure the board is adding value. But meetings must be designed to give the board the time it needs to do its real work. Though more complex companies or companies in dynamic industries might consider more frequent meetings, most boards can probably cover it all in eight meetings per year.

These meetings can't simply be morning presentations, followed by lunch. Given the external context, risk factors, macro issues, compliance issues, and all the rest, there's simply not enough time to hold meaningful dialogue between breakfast and lunch. Progressive boards set aside a full day for meetings; some may even run a day and a half each.

The meetings themselves should have agendas that build on the Twelve-Month Agenda and maximize discussion time. Directors should come to meetings with board briefings read in full and be prepared to jump right in with dialogue and questions. Several topics described in this book deserve periodic attention during board meetings. That is, the board should be sure to include on the meeting agenda discussions on the following topics:

- Balance sheet, twice per year
- Leadership gene pool and succession, twice per year
- CEO compensation, once per year
- Risk, once per year
- Strategy, once or twice per year outside of board meetings
- Crisis management, once per year

These are guidelines, not rules. And it doesn't mean these topics are not discussed at other board meetings. One company goes so far as to set up a checklist of board requirements and meetings (see Exhibit 11.2). In this way, the board can monitor over time that it is covering its responsibilities.

To develop the agenda for a particular meeting, the lead director might work with the CEO to form a preliminary agenda. Directors then provide input of their own, and the agenda is adjusted well in advance of the meeting.

Exhibit 11.2. One Board's Requirements and Meeting Schedule Checklist.

BOARD OF DIRECTORS REQUIREMENTS

	Meeting 1	Meeting 2	Meeting 3	Meeting 4	Meeting 5	Meeting 6
Board Responsibilities						
Review and approve management's strategic and business plan.		✓			☐	
Review and approve financial plans, objectives, and actions including significant capital allocations and expenditures.		✓	✓		☐	☐
Recommend director candidates for election by shareholders.		✓		☐		
Evaluate Chair/CEO and other senior executives.				☐		☐
Compensate Chair/CEO and other senior executives based on performance in meeting predetermined standards and objectives.				☐		
Review management development and succession plans.					☐	
Review procedures designed to promote compliance with laws and regulations and setting an ethical tone at the top.						

Exhibit 11.2. One Board's Requirements and Meeting Schedule Checklist, Cont'd.

	Meeting 1	Meeting 2	Meeting 3	Meeting 4	Meeting 5	Meeting 6
Review procedures designed to promote integrity and candor in the audit of the company's financial statements and operations, and in all financial reporting and disclosure.					□	
Assess the effectiveness of the board's governance practices and procedures.	✓					
Risk Management						
Appraise the company's major risks and determine that appropriate risk management and control procedures are in place.	✓	✓	✓	□	□	□
Board Organization						
The board consists of a majority of independent directors.	✓	✓	✓	□	□	□
The lead director facilitates and chairs executive sessions of the board.	✓	✓	✓	□	□	□
Board maintains three standing committees.	✓	✓	✓	□	□	□
All committees report on activities to the board.	✓	✓	✓	□	□	□
Board is normally constituted of eleven directors.	○	○	✓	□	□	□
Nominating and Governance Committee reviews the board's organization annually and recommends appropriate changes to the board.	✓	✓				

Board Meetings

- One board meeting is in conjunction with the Annual General Meeting.
- Lead director sets meeting agenda.
- Directors receive the agenda and materials for regularly scheduled meetings at least one week in advance of meeting.
- Executive session of independent non-executive directors is held at each formal meeting of the board.
- Copies of minutes are forwarded promptly to all directors after each board meeting.

Board and Committee Calendars

- A calendar of regular agenda items for the regularly scheduled board meetings is prepared.
- A calendar of regular agenda items for the regularly scheduled committee meetings is prepared.

Board Contact with Operations and Management

- One of the six meetings is in conjunction with a visit to the company's operations.
- Senior managers attend board meetings.

Board Self-Evaluation

- Board reviews annual evaluation results.

Exhibit 11.2. One Board's Requirements and Meeting Schedule Checklist, Cont'd.

	Meeting 1	Meeting 2	Meeting 3	Meeting 4	Meeting 5	Meeting 6
Lead director meets informally with each of the directors as part of evaluation.	✓					
Qualifications and performance of all board members are reviewed in connection with the renomination of the board.	✓	✓				
Board Compensation and Stock Ownership						
Compensation Committee and Nominating & Governance Committee review the directors' compensation and recommends changes to the board.				☐		
Director Service						
Directors are elected by shareholders at annual meeting.			✓			
Director Orientation and Education						
A program of continuing education is annually provided to incumbent directors.	✓	✓	✓	☐	☐	☐
Directors annually review the company's Guide to Ethical Conduct.					☐	

Other Directorships and Conflicts

Non-executive directors who are not fully employed do not serve on more than five other public company boards.	✓	✓	☐	☐	☐
Non-executive directors who are fully employed do not serve on more than three other public company boards.	✓	✓	☐	☐	☐
CEO does not serve on more than two boards of other public companies.	✓	✓	☐	☐	☐

Other

Board reviews and approves minutes from prior meeting.	✓	✓	☐	☐	☐

LEGEND

✓—Completed
○—Not Completed
☐—Proposed Agenda Item

Many directors will also assemble the night before a board meeting officially begins. They'll gather for informal meetings over dinner or cocktails with fellow directors or with management. This interaction is an essential part of forming a rich board dynamic, and an excellent chance to gauge direct reports and up-and-coming managers. These apparently social occasions serve a purpose and are a good way to jump-start the group dynamics.

| **Working with Investors**

External pressures have forced boards to change, but they cannot relinquish control of their own destiny and that of the company. As boards come of age, the thoroughness of their processes and the depth of their discussions will give them the confidence to stand firm amid conflicting demands.

The challenge is to be responsive to external constituencies but not let them replace the collective judgment of the board. Just as the board must maintain a good relationship with the CEO while maintaining an independent viewpoint, it should also listen to employees, customers, suppliers, investors—anyone who has a stake in the company—but reach its own collective conclusions about what is right for the long-term viability of the company. It can't afford to be swayed off course by vocal and persuasive third parties.

The challenge is particularly complex and requires the utmost sophistication and judgment when it comes to investors. Directors have to find mechanisms to assess what sources the board should listen to, what concerns are legitimate, and how to beware of self-interest.

Sources the Board Should Listen To

When investors pressure management to divest, restructure, pay a dividend, or make some other strategic move, the board must weigh carefully whether the complaints are legitimate. It may be helpful to consider first who is making the demand. The shareholder base is not monolithic. It is made up of many types of investors, with different motives ranging from long-term growth to short-term hedging. That dynamic makes markets efficient vehicles for raising capital. But it also confuses the definition of an investor as an *owner.*

Further muddying the water is the fact that, according to Vanguard Guard founder John Bogle (quoted on the Vanguard Web site), 56 percent of equity shares are controlled by the hundred largest institutional managers, who are actually proxies for mutual fund investors, pensioners, insurance companies, and other entities. In a sense, they are "derivative shareholders," in that their shareholder status is conferred on them by other people's money. Many of these professional managers make their bonuses based on short-term performance, which means their outlook is decidedly focused on the short term. Indeed, the average holding period for institutionally owned shares is only eleven months, according to Bogle. It is unlikely that their motives are the same as those of a true owner, one with skin in the game who is in it for the long term.

There are, however, institutional holders whose opinions matter. Some hold large blocks of stock for long periods of time. These investors may not understand the company as well as the board, but they are sophisticated businesspeople who understand the competition and the marketplace. They can tell the difference between external pressures and inadequate management, and will generally keep quiet unless they perceive serious missteps relative to the economy or competitors. So when the head of a $10 billion company fails to give an acceptable range of guidance for eight consecutive quarters, which has happened, these investors begin to gripe. That's when the board and management should listen.

Boards should interact directly with the company's Investor Relations Department to get information on investors' concerns. Some have the director of IR visit the boardroom on occasion to tell the board directly what word is coming in from investors every day. A good board makes sure top management is responsive to and communicating with these investors. That could mean pushing back, but it must be done respectfully rather than antagonistically. The CEO's credibility is very important and the board should coach the CEO if that credibility is slipping.

Likewise, the board itself needs to maintain its own credibility. Controversies will emerge; directors should develop a process to deal with them and to communicate directly with major investors, if necessary. Boards should carefully discuss how to do that without enfeebling the CEO.

One way to establish credibility over time is to open up a regular communications channel with investors. Intel has at least two directors address the annual meeting each year, on topics such as the board's audit process and executive compensation. Providing some transparency into the board's operations will help the public see that the board is working hard on its behalf.

Another way to communicate with investors is to include in the company's annual report a letter from the lead director or Governance Committee Chair, signed by all non-executive directors. Committee Chairs could write their own letters. The communiqués would outline the functioning of the board or committee, accomplishments over the past year, and the goals for the coming year. Over time, the transparency will improve the public's comfort level with the board. These practices let everyone know the board is diligent, not negligent, and listening to investors' concerns.

Legitimate Concerns

A broader range of investors are active today, and when they are dissatisfied with the company's earnings or direction, they insist on change. Investors are no longer content to vote with their wallets (that is, sell their shares) or to resort to a leveraged buyout when management and the board are unresponsive.

Serious long-term investors raise many legitimate issues that boards have to consider:

- *Forcing divestiture:* It's common for investors in struggling firms to demand that underperforming divisions be divested. For years, Motorola CEO and Chair Chris Galvin resisted the pressures of shareholders who wanted the company's semiconductor division sold. But he never made a compelling case for holding the unit, and he couldn't turn it around. He was let go late in 2003 and the company announced it would indeed spin off the semiconductor unit, even before naming Galvin's replacement.
- *Strategy:* In September 2003, Kodak CEO and Chair Dan Carp announced a plan to shift Kodak's strategy more aggressively

into digital products. As part of the strategy, the dividend was cut dramatically and $3 billion was designated for acquisitions and internal investments. Investors voiced two complaints: First, some investors wanted the company to shrink and keep the dividend. Second, other investors didn't think the company could execute its ambitious strategy. Carp spent a lot of time publicly defending the strategy approved by the board.

- *CEO:* The run-up to Disney's annual shareholders meeting in March 2004 was a prominent demonstration of investors out for a CEO's head, in this case Michael Eisner's. Pressure mounted on the board to act. The board decided not to remove Eisner, but stripped him of the Chair position.
- *Tainted director:* Directors who serve at a company where fraud is alleged become tainted, in the eyes of some investors. This was particularly true for the highest-profile corporate failures, such as Enron, whose directors came under fire in their other directorships.
- *Compensation plan:* GlaxoSmithKline had to revamp the compensation plan for CEO Jean-Pierre Garnier in 2003 after U.K. shareholders rejected a proposal that included a potentially significant severance if things didn't work out.
- *Social responsibility:* The oil majors have become lightning rods for activists who call for more responsible business practices around the world. These increasing pressures are coming not only from picketers but also from investors.
- *Dividend policy:* For many years, investors watched Microsoft build up hoards of cash—over $40 billion at the end of 2002 while it generated nearly $1 billion in free cash each month— yet the company never paid a dividend. The company finally relented by paying an annual dividend in early 2003. A substantial special dividend was announced the following year.
- *Succession:* In the United Kingdom, Fidelity Investments joined a number of shareholders in blocking the 2003 appointment of Michael Green as Chair of ITV, the merged Carlton Communications and Granada Media. In October, the board capitulated and decided to search for a new Chair.

Getting results further emboldens investors. The public campaign against management and the board of Disney in early 2004, led by former directors Roy Disney and Stanley Gold, embarrassed that board into taking action. The company was not at all near bankruptcy at the time. Indeed, the dissidents may have mistimed their battle—the company began to demonstrate far improved financial performance just as the fight began to heat up. Nevertheless, they had legitimate complaints about senior management over the preceding few years, especially about the disturbing lack of board involvement on a succession plan. The incident gave a lot of energy and publicity to other activists. "A director's willingness to say, in the boardroom, that an investor's criticism may have merit could have saved many companies and their investors untold grief over the past few years," says *Fortune*'s Colvin.

Still, while the board has to listen to investors, it sometimes must ignore what they say and help the CEO withstand their criticism. Not all vocal shareholders are serious long-term investors, as Disney and Gold were; some are chasing fads or are in it for a quick buck or for political gain. If the board believes in the company's strategy, and that the CEO is executing the correct balance of short-term and long-term objectives, it should stand behind the CEO in resisting these short-sighted pressures. A number of energy industry CEOs showed courage to stay the course when investors wanted them to follow Enron's strategy. It was a difficult period for these CEOs, but the confidence their boards showed in them paid off when Enron's flaws were exposed.

The new reality is that boards have to be sensitive to the concerns of serious long-term shareholders and at the same time filter out the shrill demands and the self-interests of short-term investors. Directors have to discern who is complaining and why, get to the heart of long-term investors' grievances, and be prepared to stand up to the rest.

Beware of Self-Interest

The Wall Street community presents issues for boards above and beyond investor relations. The world of investment bankers, equity analysts, credit analysts, and now governance analysts consists of smart businesspeople with good ideas, but it is also rife with conflicting interests. Many of these professionals have something valuable to say, but boards must consider the sources.

Governance analysts, for example, are gaining influence, despite their arguably flawed methodologies. Some of the researchers attempt to sell advice to the very companies they are rating, setting up a conflict of interest. Nevertheless, some investors are listening to the raters and putting pressure on companies based on the survey findings. The board has to be cognizant of the issues the governance analysts raise and conscious of whether their arguments are gaining any traction with mainstream investors.

Likewise, buy-side analysts have significant influence in the investor community. Their research of the industry, competitors, suppliers, and customers can be helpful to management and the board in setting the external context for strategy. It can go too far, however, when the analysts begin to make strategy recommendations—or demands.

Institutional investors share extensive social networks, the members of which are on several boards. When the investors begin to feel that a company is not performing the way they think it should, they begin to use their networks to put pressure on boards. Directors who are caught up in this activity do not often declare in their board meetings where the pressure is coming from. If other board members become aware of such situations, they should stand up to the pressures if they decide the CEO or the strategy needs to be defended.

Leveraging the Board for Competitive Advantage

The string of company meltdowns seems to have subsided for now, but it served its purpose by bringing to light issues central not only to governance but also to running a business. Stiffer penalties and new regulations may help prevent fraud, but they do not address the fundamental issue of creating value and improving the company's competitive position. Management faces increasingly complex and intense demands. Boards have a central role to play, and they must exercise it fully.

The nexus of power to run the business must be with the CEO and the board—both. The best CEOs are powerful in the good sense of the word—they have command of the business, receive input from and stand up to constituencies as necessary, address issues head on, confront strong individuals when needed, and so on.

Boards must be just as powerful in doing their job of helping management make sense of internal and external complexities and ensuring that the talk matches reality. If the CEO is incapable of running the business properly, replacement is necessary. More often, the CEO needs the board's input, coaching, and support.

Today's directors have a calling, and they must respond by continually improving their practices. Only a strong board can counterbalance the many people with influence whose desires and ambitions have been misaligned with creating intrinsic value. These influencers include those compensation consultants who have worked one-sidedly to maximize the benefits and minimize the risk to their client CEOs; some investment bankers, analysts, accountants, and consultants who have led management down the wrong path because of a short-term orientation or self-interest; and some executive search firms, the media, and vocal social constituencies, all of which have their own goals and interests.

The dedication to improvement does not mean a focus on mechanical steps or structural improvements. Those won't change the real effectiveness of a board. A director's job is intuitive, not mechanical. Yes, directors must read balance sheets and comply with Sarbanes-Oxley's myriad criteria. But the real substance of a board's work requires judgment. Directors must help each other pick up on hints, test instincts, and develop a sixth sense for landing on the important issues. There is work to be done, and satisfaction to be gained in doing it. Effective corporate governance—turning the board into a competitive advantage—is as much a reward for the participants as it is for the companies they govern.

While the practices in this book focus on directors, the CEO is, of course, a vital aspect of the board's functioning, and is instrumental in making the board Progressive. As I wrote this book, I kept recalling the conversation I had with Jim Doyle, the CEO described in the first chapter. His board is in many ways typical of a Liberated board. That is to say, Jim has turned to his board for help and the directors are active participants in governance—but the board has not yet become all that it could and should be. CEOs have so much to gain by helping their boards become Progressive. So I decided to write Jim the following note to encourage him to continue to improve governance at his company. No doubt the message applies to many other CEOs as well, and if they take it to heart, significant changes will take place quickly.

> Dear Jim:
>
> I have been reflecting for some time now on the conversation we had. Almost a year has passed, during which I have done much research and analysis. So many boards, like yours, are going through this phase of Liberation. Some, but not all, are making deliberate progress toward the transition to Progressive.
>
> There is an opportunity here for every CEO to make the board a competitive advantage. My view is that you should consider getting together with the Chair of your Governance Committee and your lead

director, and accept the challenge for the three of you to make your board Progressive. I believe if you consider the following few points and methodically create a plan to guide the board, yours could become a board potential directors would love to join in the future, and against which other boards will be compared:

- Discuss among the three of you what will make the dialogue productive; then sit with the whole board and decide on the rules of engagement for the board going forward. By explicitly talking about the need for consensus and closure, the directors will individually see how they contribute to the group dynamics. Jointly determining a Twelve-Month Agenda will help the group stay focused on key issues.

- Have an ad hoc committee sit with you and your CFO to talk about an information architecture that helps the board understand the business and how it makes money. It will save meeting time for dialogue. It may take a few iterations to get the package right, but the improved productivity of the board makes it well worth the effort.

- Design a strategy immersion session different from the retreat that you held. You and your team should personally present the strategy and leave plenty of time for a lively discussion. It's a great way to get all the directors on board and give the board the proper context for future decisions that will come to them for approval (remember, that's why the GE board could quickly approve acquisitions following their 2003 off-site). Not having a clear consensus on strategy will hamstring the board and make your job harder. If the immersion session doesn't achieve consensus on strategic direction, consider developing a strategy blueprint to follow up.

- Warren Buffett has called CEO pay the "acid test" for boards. The issue is certainly picking up steam. Make sure that the Compensation Committee has carefully considered the philosophy and the range of behaviors that will make the business better and that it works with the full board to establish multiple objectives for you and your team. Creating a compensation framework will help link the objectives with specific forms of pay. That should make you and the board more comfortable with the public's increased demands for transparency.

- You are only fifty-three, Jim, so succession is not an immediate issue. However, you and your board need to begin planning for that day now and for the possibility of an emergency succession. How rich is the leadership gene pool at your company? Do the directors know the criteria through which the leadership gene pool is being selected and developed? Have the directors begun to meet the next generation of leaders? Focusing on these issues now will pay huge dividends down the road.

No doubt your board wants to contribute. They want you and the company to be successful. It is up to you to take the lead, and indicate that you would love to have them contribute to shareholder value creation and the longevity of the company. If you are able to transform your board, it will free up a lot of time so you can devote your energy to other management issues. And I think that you will find your board, once it has become Progressive, will be a nourishing source of ideas and support. Your psychological energy will be renewed, and you will be able to tell your friends that you have the best, most thought-provoking, most helpful board in the world.

I've seen committee heads and lead directors initiate these kinds of improvements in how the board functions, but there's no reason a CEO can't lead the charge, as Jeff Immelt did at GE. Leaders are leaders. Jim, I think you are a great leader and you have other great leaders on the board. Together, you can take corporate governance—and the company—to the next level.

Best regards,
Ram Charan

Appendix A:
Sample Strategy Blueprint

This is an example of a strategy blueprint that was published in a company's annual report. It contains enough content to provoke dialogue between the board and management regarding the proposed strategy. It is a very good platform for shaping the discussion around questions like: How realistic is the strategy? What are the risks? What was missed? What is overemphasized? Under what conditions will it deliver, or not deliver, results? What will it take to execute? Through such questions, directors can help shape the strategy.

Excerpt from NDC Health 2003 Annual Report

There are three key elements to our strategy: to increase revenue per claim through value added transactions, to grow claims volume as healthcare grows and through gains in market share, and to take full advantage of our extensive claims processing resources in our information management business in order to be well positioned for a rebound in the pharmaceutical manufacturing industry. The United States Government estimates that of the $1.5 trillion spent on healthcare in the U.S., 66% is spent on administration and inappropriate care. We believe we play an important role in providing automation, transaction processing, and information solutions to improve the efficiency and efficacy of healthcare.

Our strategy starts with the fundamental transaction in healthcare's revenue cycle—the submission of claims from providers to third party payers. We estimate that we process approximately 45% of these electronic healthcare claims in the United States. Our revenue increases as we gain market share and provide advanced edit processing and other value-added products and services to the

177

claims in real-time to add significant customer value. We are able to price incrementally for these additional products and services in addition to the pricing for the base claim. Further, due to an aging population and increasing automation in healthcare, the claims volume grows, also increasing revenue.

From our network, we capture the claim and related transaction information, combine that information with data we purchase, and create valuable information solutions for pharmaceutical manufacturers and providers, such as pharmacies. Our information strategy is to continue to aggregate and integrate data from our processing network to create unique new products which build additional streams of revenue and expand margins. We also have an international expansion strategy to further leverage our proven business model.

Today, we provide products and services to four major areas of the healthcare industry: pharmacies (retail, mail order, Internet based and specialty), hospitals, physicians, and pharmaceutical manufacturers. By aggregating and integrating data from the three provider markets we increasingly create unique business insights for pharmaceutical manufacturers, or pharma. Our goal, as healthcare evolves, is to also expand our customer base to include payers, employers and consumers while reducing the effective cost per unit of data.

Building Blocks

The first and central building block of our business is being the primary information service company for the three major components of the pharmacy industry's technology infrastructure. For pharmacies, we: (1) provide systems that optimize the prescription fulfillment process, the labor intensive element of the pharmacy business, (2) provide a value-added claims processing and real-time edit processing network that we believe has the highest performance, quality, and integrity in transaction processing, and (3) provide the data warehouse/analytical capabilities that can produce unique business management insights to pharmacy customers.

We believe we are the only company capable of integrating all three of these pharmacy technology functions to optimize our customers' business models. In the financial and administrative areas we add value applications as diverse as workflow efficiency, pricing, product substitution, regulatory compliance, and loss prevention. In the area of workflow efficiency for example, our solutions permit the prescription fulfillment process to allow parallel rather than sequential processing. This allows multiple specialists, often at different locations, to contribute to filling the prescription, resulting in a requirement for fewer pharmacists, currently in scarce supply, and greater throughput. Our customers benefit from needing fewer people, reduced hiring and training requirements, and lower inventory levels with more turns.

In fiscal 2003, we also moved into the clinical application area with NDC Rx Safety Advisor, an application we believe will further differentiate us from our competitors. Our pharmacy application solutions directly affect a pharmacy's cash flow and margins.

The acquisition of TechRx has strengthened our position in the key point-of-service prescription fulfillment area. Our strategy with TechRx's new line of point-of-sale products is to convert the TechRx revenue model to a transaction based model to create a recurring revenue stream.

The next major building block is claims processing for hospitals, as well as providing claims editing to increase the acceptance rate by payers of hospital claims and assist hospital management in improving cash flow and reducing outstanding accounts receivable. NDC ePREMIS, a new platform for revenue cycle management launched in fiscal 2003, incorporates new technology, expands functional attributes, and creates the base upon which new applications can be built. This expands our opportunity to increase revenue by providing a broader suite of integrated services to customers. This offering, using new application Internet technology, allows us to upgrade our existing base of over 1,500 hospital customers, add new large hospitals and provides the opportunity to penetrate a new market strata, small hospitals under 100 beds. Similar to our pharmacy offerings, the new workflow features of this offering permit multiple people to work with claims simultaneously, yielding greater efficiency and better workload balancing. NDC ePREMIS can also be integrated into hospital information systems provided by various major companies to further extend our market reach.

The third building block is the niche we have created in the physician market space. We have sold our solutions to more than 100,000 physicians primarily in the 1–3 physician practice group market. Physicians' offices utilize our software and systems to do patient scheduling, billing and manage accounts receivables. Because of the relative lack of automation in small physician offices, we believe these customers represent a unique opportunity for expanded electronic service. This electronic connection also assists our customers in improving their cash flow and provides an important communication channel to the physician. We have already connected systems for 13,000 physicians to an on-line network for electronic claims processing. Additionally, in conjunction with our pharmacy network and services, the predicted growth of e-prescribing provides an important opportunity for us to become a leader in this emerging application area.

These three markets enable us to create access to data to develop applications for the fourth building block—on-line, value-added information products primarily for pharmaceutical manufacturing companies. By capturing claims and related transaction information through our network and combining it with purchased data, we can utilize our data analysis and data warehousing resources to allow our pharma customers to enhance their prescriber targeting capability, optimize sales force assignments, determine sales compensation, and enhance competitiveness and margins. In addition, by providing pharma customers with access to the capabilities of our value-added pharmacy, hospital and physician networks, we are in a position to provide drug tracking to help eliminate counterfeit medicines and timely messages to assist patients and providers in enhancing the efficacy of their drug treatment.

In fiscal 2003, our share of the healthcare pharmaceutical information market was approximately 30% in the United States, based on the number of pharmaceutical sales representatives compensated utilizing our products, and we have a small partnership in the United Kingdom and a presence in Germany. In fiscal 2003, the pharmaceutical industry is faced with a slowing of new drug introductions. Industry analysts anticipate new drug introductions will accelerate in 2005 or 2006. In the interim, there will be pressure on our revenues from this group of customers. In the near term, domestic revenues in this market are likely to remain relatively flat, a result of the cyclical downturn in the pharmaceutical industry. We are committed to the information business and the pharma industry and will continue to invest in and manage the quality and cost effectiveness of our current applications. At the same time we intend to move into new areas of opportunity in which we can leverage our claims transaction processing to be a unique provider of insightful, value-adding applications. We believe these actions will position us well for the future.

Eight Quarter Plan

We have developed an eight quarter operating plan which has three key priorities: 1) focus on revenue growth; 2) control operational and administrative costs to realize margin improvement; and 3) generate significant cash to reduce debt.

In the next eight quarters, our plan calls for:

- Generation of more than $100 million in free cash flow, defined as net cash generated by operating activities less capital expenditures and dividends;
- Reduction in levels of debt, thus reducing interest expense and lowering our debt to capital ratio toward a target of 35%;
- Low double-digit to mid-teens revenue growth in both business segments by the fourth quarter of fiscal 2005;
- Operating margin expansion of more than 100 basis points by the fourth quarter of fiscal 2005 compared to the fourth quarter of fiscal 2003;
- Continued investment in new products and services focusing on four key development initiatives, which are: developing the next generation pharmacy and mail-order system platforms; building our unique Medical Repository database containing longitudinal data elements from all of healthcare; penetrating the growing market for electronic prescriptions; and gaining critical mass in European operations to achieve profitability.

Appendix B:
The Research Agenda

For as long as the stock market has existed, researchers have tried to unravel it by making correlations with everything from complex combinations of economic variables to the length of women's hemlines and who wins the Super Bowl. When cause-and-effect is conspicuously missing, the theories can be quite humorous. Does anyone really believe that miniskirts cause a bull market? The point is that making a statistical correlation is very different from proving cause and effect.

Unfortunately, most academic research on corporate governance is based on statistical correlations, not on causal relationships. The researchers are intellectually honest, and they often point out that their conclusions are tentative and that the correlations don't imply causality. But the media and board watchers often seize upon the correlations as causal factors and use them as spurious prescriptions for all boards. For example, it's a tenuous, unproven assumption that "director independence," in any one of its many definitions, is at all related to improved corporate performance, yet it is recommended as a universal fix for boards of all shapes and forms. The same goes for variables such as directors' stock ownership, the CEO and Chair being different individuals, or the number of meetings held.

For the most part, governance research is limited to accessible statistical data that researchers can sift through in their attempt to find associations between variables. They typically rely on information from secondary sources such as proxy filings, Standard & Poor's Compustat, Register of Corporations and ExecuComp databases, the Corporate Library's Board Analyst database, the *Forbes* annual executive survey, and the *Dun & Bradstreet Reference Book of Corporate Management,* among others. Some firms survey current practices to determine recommendations, but, again, their findings are not based on actual boardroom behavior. No matter how sophisticated the math, such research misses how directors actually interact, work together, and contribute.

Board watchers and some investors use the ambiguous conclusions of corporate governance research to argue for change in boardrooms. But when they make demands like removing Warren Buffett from the board of Coca-Cola, they are clearly placing too much import on countable variables and not enough on the individuals and their collective behaviors.

A New Research Agenda

The time is ripe for a new, more useful strand of research into corporate governance that takes a hard look into the behavioral factors that make boards effective. Extracting meaningful lessons for boards requires a longitudinal, multidisciplinary approach to studying governance—one that is careful in establishing causal relationships and that tracks board practices and corporate performance over time. Good research along these lines will yield an improvement of practices at all corporations.

The research agenda needs to move from statistical number-crunching to primary research based on clinical observation. The starting point is to identify key decisions made by particular boards: the appointment of a CEO, for example, or a significant shift in strategy. In fact, researchers should examine decisions made in the five contributions that count—the right CEO and succession, CEO compensation, the right strategy, the leadership gene pool, and monitoring health, performance, and risk. From my experience, I posit that the right CEO and succession is the decision that accounts for the largest component of corporate performance, possibly up to 60 percent. But all the contributions affect the company's long-term health considerably.

From each key decision, researchers should work backward in time to determine the board practices and processes that went into the decision. This will require interviews and observations to determine precisely how the board came to its decision. The case sample should be revisited and the interviewees re-interviewed over the course of a few years; the longitudinal pattern of interviews and researchers' observations will reveal how practices inside the boardroom influence corporate performance over time. Directors may stress different elements of the process and have different views of what actually transpired, so the researchers must carefully cross-check the findings through multiple interviews with different directors, and use judgment to determine an objective sense of what really happened.

Then the researchers should work forward in time to determine the performance of the company—understanding that there is a time lag between when a decision is made and when true outcomes are known. A great new CEO takes time to master the situation and deliver results that are visible and sustainable. Development efforts to strengthen a leadership gene pool could take a dozen years to show benefits. But they will.

From this deeper level of inquiry over a sample of perhaps a dozen companies, a set of principles will emerge and a framework can be developed that will delineate the conditions under which the principles will hold.

This is not a simple project to be left to a business school Ph.D. candidate. The research team will require a highly skilled interviewer, perhaps from an organizational behavior background, to extract the views of a number of board members for each particular company studied—with candor and care to value the confidence of the interviewee and the corporation. The interviewer would need expertise in analyzing group dynamics, experience in conducting clinical research on high-level executives, and the mental bandwidth to understand the breadth of corporate decision making at the highest level.

The team will also require a seasoned researcher who can separate corporate performance related to the key decision from effects attributable to other circumstances. This need probably calls for an individual with a finance background, someone who can carve out the different drivers of financial performance relative to competitors, including shifts in the economy, changes in market demand, financial engineering, or the effects of the key decision under study. A singular focus on the stock price will not yield an accurate picture of corporate performance.

A Framework of Practices for Good Governance

Deep research on a smaller sample of companies will uncover the practices that can be shown to produce results—it will expose the causal factors that link good governance with good performance. But even the best output can not be generalized to all situations. For example, if a company has a very effective Governance Committee Chair with balanced roles between the CEO and Chair, it might not need a lead director to maintain effective group dynamics, even if a lead director has proved effective elsewhere. The practices are not one-size-fits-all; they will yield positive outcomes more often than not—but there is likely to be more than one way to achieve the same objective.

The research team must place a framework around its findings to define the boundary conditions under which each identified practice is likely to be relevant. Outside those conditions, all bets are off. Some of those conditions could be characteristics of the board. Others could be conditions at the company, such as a high debt/equity ratio, or outside the company, such as a recession.

The combination of interview-based corporate governance data, firsthand observations, and realistic corporate performance data will yield a far more meaningful peek into the reality of what's happening in boardrooms. It's not useful to measure whether a board made a good decision to hire a CEO, for example, by counting the hours spent in executive sessions and correlating it to stock performance in the first year in office. More useful would be interviews that drill down into how robust was the thinking by which the board selected the CEO. Did the directors begin discussions two years in advance of succession? Ten years in advance? How well-defined were the selection criteria? How rigorous was the interview process? Was the outgoing CEO involved? How did the board direct the executive search firm? Then researchers must allow some time to pass before measuring the impact of the decision.

The sample size need not be big. From deep research of a small number of companies, the winning combination of practices will become evident. As clinical research details the true causal relationships and their relative importance, it can influence how boards direct their attention, and thus can radically improve both corporate governance and company performance.

Acknowledgments

This book is for corporate boards, executives, and advisors—but it is also *from* them. I have been privileged over many, many years to learn from some of the best in the business. It was truly an honor to have so many boards make themselves available to me.

Along the way, many individuals have also shown a gracious willingness to share with me their great insights on boards and have given me the time to test the ideas in this book. There are too many to fit in this space, but they include, alphabetically, Geoff Beattie, Larry Bossidy, Ed Breen, Jack Breen, Dick Brown, Jose Carrion, Richard Carrion, Bill Conaty, David Cote, Dennis Donovan, David Fuente, Gordon Fyfe, Harvey Golub, Robert Guido, Raj Gupta, Dick Harrington, Ben Heineman, Walter Hoff, Chad Holliday, Vester Hughes, Jeff Immelt, Clark Johnson, Greg Josefowicz, Mano Kampouris, Roger Kenny, Don Keough, John Koster, Jack Krol, George Lorch, John Luke, Gary Malloy, Jack Mollen, Jim Mulva, David Murphy, Bob Nardelli, Lars Nyberg, Dean O'Hare, Eric Pillmore, Jim Reda, William Rhodes, Mike Ruettgers, Hellene Runtagh, John Sasen, Ivan Seidenberg, David Smith, Jim Smith, Bill Solomon, Don Stewart, Joe Viviano, Patrick Wang, Larry Weinbach, Bob Weissman, Wendell Willkie, and Ed Woolard. All of you deserve special acknowledgment.

I also have to thank *Fortune*'s Geoff Colvin, who opened my eyes to the need for a book on this topic. It was you, Geoff, who started me on this journey six years ago after John Huey recommended that you help me with the outline for *Boards at Work*, my first book on corporate governance. It has been a great partnership ever since, as we wrote articles together and co-hosted Fortune Boardroom Forums. And it has been a great friendship, as well.

Geri Willigan, my trusted partner for twelve years, helped me break ground on corporate governance with *Boards at Work*. Ever since, she has been integral to my editorial endeavors to improve the practice of business leadership, in general, and corporate governance, in particular. Geri played a key role in shaping this book, from idea stage to final copy, helping me draw out from a huge amount of disparate information the core lessons for building an effective board of directors. Her sharp analytical skills, deep content knowledge, and keen editorial instincts gave this book the clarity, structure, and focus the audience deserves.

Larry Yu was the point man in crafting a user-friendly manuscript and gathering background information and research materials. He tenaciously mastered the topic and meticulously searched for and integrated important insights from numerous sources, including the interviews we conducted together. Larry also worked diligently and creatively to put the ideas in clear, succinct language that respects readers' time and intelligence. He is a great team player whose engagement with the topic improved the book at every turn.

Susan Williams and her colleagues at Jossey-Bass were great (and flexible) shepherds of the project. They are true professionals who gave me unqualified support while setting high standards on behalf of readers.

Thanks also to John Joyce, my lifelong business partner, who always has encouragement for me and takes the time to read every draft. John helps keep me grounded in practicality and common sense.

Cynthia Burr and Carol Davis did their usual heroics in providing the administrative and logistical help needed to keep the project on track. I am grateful for their ongoing dedication and support.

About the Author

Ram Charan is an adviser, author, and teacher famous among directors and senior executives for his practical solutions to complex business and boardroom problems. For more than thirty-five years, he has worked behind the scenes at some of the world's most successful companies, including GE, Verizon, Novartis, Du Pont, Thomson, Honeywell, KLM, Bank of America, Home Depot, and Johnson Electric Hong Kong. He has helped numerous boards transform their practices by facilitating board retreats, assisting with board evaluations, and providing guidance on succession issues.

Dr. Charan has numerous books to his credit, including the best-sellers *Confronting Reality: Doing What Matters to Get Things Right* and *Execution: The Discipline of Getting Things Done* (both coauthored with Larry Bossidy), *Profitable Growth,* and *What the CEO Wants You to Know.* His past writing on corporate governance includes *Boards at Work* and articles for *Strategy+Business, Director's Monthly, Directorship, Directors and Officers,* and *Corporate Board.*

Dr. Charan's energetic, interactive teaching style has won him the Bell Ringer award at GE's famous Crotonville Institute and best teacher award at Northwestern. He was among *BusinessWeek*'s Top 10 Resources for in-house executive development programs.

Dr. Charan has MBA and doctorate degrees from Harvard Business School, where he graduated with high distinction with a specialty in corporate governance and later served on the faculty. He has served as co-host of the Fortune Boardroom Forum and on the Blue Ribbon Commission on Corporate Governance. He is on the board of Austin Industries. Dr. Charan is based in Dallas, Texas.

Index

A

Accounting expertise, on board, 152, 155

Accounting figures, 66, 107. *See also* Financial measures

Ace Insurance, 35

Acquisitions and mergers: integration issues in, 56–57; strategy and, 117–118, 120

Ad hoc committees, 158

Adelphia, 8

Administrative details: best practices in, 151–166; time allocation for, 61, 69. *See also* Board operations

Agenda: board, 61–71; executive session, 38–39; meeting, 160–165; Twelve-Month, 62, 67–71, 124, 175. *See also* Focus on substantive issues

Airlines, 146

Akers, J., 76

AlliedSignal, 129–130, 132

American Association of Retired Persons (AARP), 105

American Express, 8, 107

American Standard, 130

Amersham, 117–118

Analysts, 52–53, 171, 172, 173–174

Anheuser-Busch, 117

AOL-Time Warner merger, 117

Apple Computer, 76

AT&T, 8, 102, 130, 132, 140

Audit Committee, 158; information exchange by, 59; Sarbanes-Oxley provisions on, 8; strategy and, 124

Auditors, as information sources, 59

Automakers, 143

B

Baby Bells, 102

Background-checking: of board candidates, 155–156; of CEO candidates, 84–85

Bad news: honesty about, 54, 66; as top board concern, 66

Balance sheet analysis, 142–143, 160

Banco Popular, 54, 145

Bank of America, 78

Bank of New York, 122

Bank One, 82

BankAmerica, 78

Banks, 117

Behavioral norms, 30–32

Bell, C., 71, 85

Benchmarks, 52, 144

Benefits, 106, 112

BlackBerries, 31

Board(s): composition of, 151–156; continuing education of, 158–159; emerging challenges to, 5–6; evolutionary phases of, 6–13, 15–22; failures of, 5–6; transition in, 5–10, 174–176. *See also* Ceremonial boards; Liberated boards; Progressive boards

Board briefing, 48, 50–54

Board-CEO relationship. *See* CEO-board relationship

Board evaluation. *See* Self-evaluation

Board leadership, 29, 32–36. *See also* Lead director

Board members. *See* Directors
Board operations, 151–166
Board watchers, 183–184
Boardroom presentations, by potential executives, 80–81, 136–137
Bogle, J., 168
Bonuses: cash, 101, 102, 110; signing, 110–111
Bookstore chain, 51–52
Bossidy, L., 130
Brand equity decline, 53, 144
Brazil, risk conditions in, 146
Breakout groups, strategy, 122–123
Breen, E., 35–36
Briefings: board, 48, 50–54; committee, 59–60
Buffett, W., 42, 65, 117, 175, 184
Building blocks, for Progressive boards, 15–22. *See also* Focus on substantive issues; Group dynamics; Information architecture
Burlington Northern, 82
Business mix, 115
BusinessWeek, 8, 26
Buy-side analysts, 172

C

Calpers, 8
Campbell Soup, 107
Candidates, board: criteria for, 152–154; finding and assessing, 154–156
Candidates, CEO: for emergency succession, 85–86; insider, getting to know, 79–82, 135–138; leadership gene pool and, 129–138; outsider, assessing, 83–86. *See also* CEO selection; Succession plan and process
Canon, 127
Cantalupo, J., 71
Capital structure, financial health diagnosis and, 142–143
Career growth opportunities, 135
Carlton Communications, 170
Carp, D., 169–170
Carrion, J., 145, 147

Cash bonuses, 101, 102, 110
Cash component, of CEO compensation, 101–102, 104–108
Cash flow: information about, 51; monitoring financial health and, 65, 142; performance objectives and, 100–101
Causal relationships, research on, 26, 183–186
Cell phones, 31
Ceremonial boards: characteristics of, 6, 7; focus on substantive issues in, 17; group dynamics in, 16, 18, 30; information architecture in, 17, 49
Chair: chief executive officer as, 156–157; as facilitator, 33; responsibilities of lead director *versus*, 35–36, 37; role of, 156–157. *See also* Chief executive officer; Lead director
Chief executive officer (CEO): in Chair role, 156–157; credibility of, with investors, 168; direct reports of, review of, 135, 136; evaluation of, 87, 91, 106–110; faltering, 92–93; feedback to, 32, 40–41, 87–92, 93; investor concerns about, 170–171; outgoing, on board, 86; retired, on board, 152; right, ensuring the, 62, 75–93; role of, in director selection, 156; role of, in successor selection, 75–76, 80; role of, in transition to Progressive board, 174–176; strategy blueprint from, 125–127; in strategy immersion session, 120–121; supporting a new, 86; termination of, 92–93; Twelve-Month Agenda setting with, 70, 175
CEO-board relationship: in Ceremonial boards, 18; division of responsibilities in, 35–36, 37, 183; executive sessions and, 36, 37, 39–41; with independent directors, 25–26; information sharing

in, 42, 47–60, 51, 87–92; lead director and, 35–36, 37; in Liberated boards, 18–19; with new chief executive officer, 86; power shift in, after Sarbanes-Oxley Act, 3–5; in Progressive boards, 19, 20, 35–36; strategy blueprint and, 125–127; time management and, 68; in transition to Progressive phase, 174–176

CEO compensation, 23–24, 94–112, 175–176; annual meetings about, 160; audit of, 107–110; board education in, 159; cash component of, 101–102, 104–106; consultants on, 111–112, 173; equity component of, 101, 102–106; framework for, 104–106; investor concerns about, 170; pay-for-performance schemes of, 94, 98, 101; performance evaluation for, 87, 91, 106–110; performance objectives and, 63, 94, 98–101, 104–106; philosophy for, defining, 95–98, 124; public scrutiny of, 94, 106, 110; repayment of, 102; severance, 110–111; tasks for setting, 95; as top board question, 63

CEO Feedback Instrument, 87, 88–90

CEO selection, 23, 75–93; assessing candidates for, 83–86; criteria definition for, 77–79, 83–84; getting to know insider candidates for, 79–82, 135–138; by Liberated boards, 75–76; practices for, 76–86; as top question for board, 62–63. *See also* Succession plan and process

China, doing business in, 97, 124, 131

Cisco, 92

Citicorp, 129

Clean slate, 86

Cliques, 20

Closure, of board meetings, 31–32

Coalitions, 20

Coca-Cola Company, 117, 184

Cognizant, 50

Colgate, 129, 132

Collins, A., 82

Colvin, G., 7, 171

Combined Code, 156–157

Comcast, 102

Committees: number and types of, 157–158; reports from, 49, 59–60; rotating Chairs or membership of, 158; strategy and, 124. *See also* Audit Committee; Compensation Committee; Governance Committee; Nominating Committee; Risk Committee

Commodity companies, CEO compensation in, 101

Communication: of bad news, 54, 66; of executive session outcomes, 32, 39–41; information architecture for, 47–60; with investors, 168–169; about Top Ten Questions, 67. *See also* Dialogue; Information architecture; Reports

Compaq, 53

Compensation, CEO. *See* CEO compensation

Compensation, undifferentiated, 135

Compensation audit, 107–110

Compensation Committee, 158; challenge to, 94; CEO performance evaluation with, 106, 107; compensation consultants and, 112; compensation philosophy and, 97–98, 124, 175–176; reports from, 59; severance issues and, 110–111

Compensation consultants, 111–112, 173

Compensation philosophy, 95–98, 124

Competition, internal, 82

Competitive advantage: leveraging the board for, 173–176; of Progressive boards, 10

Competitive environment: information on, in board briefing, 52; leadership competencies and, 132; strategy and, 115, 120, 125; as top board concern, 64. *See also* External environment

Compliance role and work: Ceremonial boards and, 7; delegation of, to committees, 59; monitoring for, 139; time allocation for, 22, 61, 69

Confidentiality, 41, 92

Conflicts of interest, 171–172

Conseco, 140

Consultants, outside, 71; compensation, 111–112; counterbalancing, 173–174; strategy, 119, 120–121, 122

Contingency plans, 25

Continuing education, for boards, 158–159

Conversations: with potential CEO candidates, 81; about Top Ten Questions, 67. *See also* Dialogue

Corporate Library, Board Analyst database, 183

Creative Artists Agency, 110

Credibility, with investors, 168–169

Credit rating, 142

Crises: annual meetings about, 160; place for, in agenda, 69–71; reward for handling, 110

Cronyism, 26

Culture, organizational: employee surveys about, 56–57; leadership development and, 138; leadership gene pool and, 130

Current information, in management letter, 55

Customer satisfaction, 143

D

Daft, D., 117

Debt: compensation philosophy and level of, 97; financial health and, 141, 142; information about, in board briefing, 52, 53; monitoring, as top board concern, 25, 65–66, 139; risk and, 145

Dell, 53, 127

Derivative shareholders, 168

Devil's advocate, 33

Diagnostic questionnaire, 11–13

Dialogue, boardroom: group dynamics in, 16–20, 29–46; hijacking of, 15; lead director facilitation of, 32–34; nitpicking in, 15, 67–68; in Progressive *versus* other boards, 14–15; rules of engagement for, 30–32, 46

Dick's Sporting Goods, 97

Digital Equipment Corporation, 76

Dimon, J., 82

Director outreach, 49, 57–59

Directors: chief executive officers as, 86, 152; continuing education for, 158–159; criteria for, 151–154; dissenting, 45; finding and assessing, 154–156; with group dynamics skills, 154–156; independent, 25–26, 183; informal interaction among, 166; of information, 49; investor concerns about, 170; peer evaluation of, 42, 44; site visits by, 57–58, 138; tainted, 170; unwanted, 30, 45–46, 155. *See also* Lead director

Discipline, 70

Discount retailer case example, of matching performance and compensation, 99–100, 105–106

Disney, R., 171

Disney, 110, 159, 170–171

Dissenting directors, 45

Diversity: in board, 152–154; in CEO succession pool, 81–82, 132–133; in leadership gene pool, 132–133

Divestiture, 169

Dividend policy, investor concerns about, 170

Donovan, D., 99

Dot-com bust, 5, 6, 70, 92, 139, 140, 146
Dow Jones, 107
DuPont, 35, 122
Dun & Bradstreet, 50
Dun & Bradstreet Reference Book of Corporate Management, 183
Dunlap, A., 76

E

E-mail, 55–56
Economics field, 98
Effectiveness, of Liberated boards, 8–9
Einstein, A., 25
Eisner, M., 170–171
EMC, 33, 131
Emergency succession, 70–71, 85–86, 176
Emerging issues, 55
Emerson Electric, 129, 133
Employee surveys, 49, 56–57
Enron, 8, 156, 170, 171
Environmental Committee, 158
Epson, 127
Equity analysts, 52–53
Equity awards, 101, 102–106
Evaluation: board, 10, 30, 42–44; CEO, 87, 91, 106–110
Evolution, board. *See* Phases of board evolution
ExecuComp, 183
Executive search firms, 75–76, 85, 174
Executive sessions, 29, 36–41; closure of, 32; management and, 36, 37, 39–41; problems with, 36, 38; productivity of, as top board concern, 66; topic selection for, 38–39
External constituencies, 149, 167, 173–174. *See also* Investors
External environment: compensation mix and, 101, 102–103; information reports on, 52, 55; leadership competencies and, 132; strategy

and, 115, 116–119, 120, 125; as top board question, 64. *See also* Competitive environment

F

Facilitator, board meeting. *See* Lead director
Facilitator, strategy immersion session, 120–121
Familial ties, 25–26
FCC regulations, 55
FDA regulations, 55
Feedback, to chief executive officer: to ensure right leadership, 87–92; from executive session, 32, 40–41; on strategy blueprint, 126–127; who is faltering, 93
Fidelity Investments, 170
Financial health monitoring, 25, 140–143; board education for, 158; diagnostics for, 142–143; practices in, 140–143; as top board concern, 65–66, 139
Financial information: in board briefing, 50, 51–53; management commentary on, 53–54
Financial markets, education about, 159
Financial measures, 25, 65–66; for diagnosing financial health, 142–143; for performance evaluation, 107; performance indicators and, 66; for strategy monitoring, 127–128
Financial models, 53
Financial Times, 26
FleetBoston, 78
Focus on substantive issues, 15, 22, 61–71; in Ceremonial boards, 17; diagnostic on, 13; in Liberated boards, 17; need for, 61–62, 67–68; in Progressive *versus* other boards, 17, 22, 61–71; Ten Questions Every Director Should Ask framework for, 61, 62–67; Twelve-Month Agenda for, 62, 67–71, 124, 175

Forbes annual executive survey, 183
Fortune Boardroom Forum, 7
Fortune magazine, 7, 8, 9, 59, 171
Founding families, 26
Fraud, 5, 170
FTC regulations, 55
Fuente, D., 97–98

G

Galvin, C., 169
Garnier, J.-P., 170
Gatorade, 117
General Electric (GE) / board of
    directors: agenda setting of, 70;
    CEO-board relationship of, 19,
    176; CEO compensation policy
    of, 103–104, 142; CEO selection
    and, 79, 80, 86; group-dynamic
    practices of, 29, 43–44; informa-
    tion architecture of, 48; leader-
    ship development of, 129, 132,
    134; as Progressive, 10; self-
    evaluation interviews of, 43–44;
    site visits of, 57, 81; strategy work
    of, 117–118, 120, 122, 175
General Foods, 129
General Motors, "Guidelines of Cor-
    porate Governance," 8
Geographic expertise, on board, 152
Geographical risk, 146
George, B., 82
Gerstner, L., 76
Ghoshal, S., 26
GlaxoSmithKline, 170
Gold, S., 171
Golub, H., 107–110
Governance analysts, 171, 172
Governance Committee, 157–158;
    board-member criteria review by,
    151–152
Governance Committee Chair: CEO
    performance review with, 87, 91,
    106; as facilitator, 33; Twelve-
    Month Agenda setting with, 70;
    unwanted directors and, 46
Granada Media, 170

Grasso, R., 94
"Grasso Effect," 106
Green, M., 170
Grinstein, G., 82
Gross margin, 51–52
Group dynamics, 15, 16–20, 29–46,
    175; board candidate skills in,
    154–155; board operations and,
    151; in Ceremonial boards, 16,
    17, 18, 30; diagnostic on, 11–12;
    information overload and, 48; in
    Liberated boards, 16, 17, 18–19,
    30, 33; practices for, 29–46; in
    Progressive *versus* other boards,
    16–20; small-group, 122–123; in
    strategy immersion sessions,
    121–122
Grove, A., 9
Growth: liquidity *versus*, 140–143;
    organic, 64–65, 152; sources of,
    64–65; as top board question,
    64–65

H

Harrison, W., 82
HealthSouth, 8
Hedging, 167–169
Hewlett-Packard, 127
High-tech companies, 52, 92, 124;
    CEO compensation in, 101; liq-
    uidity of, 139, 140, 146
Home Depot, 57, 86, 99, 105, 129,
    138
Honesty: about bad news, 54; in
    feedback to chief executive offi-
    cer, 40–41, 92; in management's
    board briefing, 54
Honeywell, 82
Human resources: compensation
    philosophy and, 97; development
    of, as top board concern, 65; in-
    formation briefings on, 52; strat-
    egy and, 116; time allocation for,
    69. *See also* Leadership gene pool
Human resources (HR) department,
    111

I

IBM, 8, 76, 130
Immelt, J., 19, 29, 48, 70, 79,
    103–104, 120, 142, 176
IMS Health, 50
Independent directors, 25–26, 183;
    CEO relationship with, 25–26
Informal contact: among directors,
    166; with below-CEO-level lead-
    ers, 50, 81, 136; for information
    exchange, 49–50, 59
Information architecture, 15, 20–22,
    47–60, 175; in Ceremonial boards,
    17, 49; channels of, 48–49, 50–60;
    defined, 48; designing, 48–50;
    diagnostic on, 12–13; in Liber-
    ated boards, 17, 21, 47–48, 51;
    need for, 20–21, 47–48; operat-
    ing performance measures in,
    144; in Progressive *versus* other
    boards, 17, 20–22, 47–60; strategy
    and, 124. *See also* Report formats;
    Reports
Information directors, 49
Information overload, 47–48, 53, 60
Information sharing, formal. *See*
    Communication; Information
    architecture; Report formats;
    Reports
Information sharing, informal,
    49–50, 59
Information sources: for research on
    boards and governance, 183–184;
    third-party, 52–53
Insurance companies, 117
Intel, 9; acquisition decision of, 120;
    information architecture of, 57,
    58, 59; investor communications
    of, 169; leadership development
    at, 129; site visits of, 57, 58; tech-
    nology seminars of, 159
Internal CEO candidates, 79–82;
    leadership gene pool for, 129–138
Internal competition, 82
Interviews: board candidate,
    155–156; CEO candidate, 84–85;
director evaluation, 43–44; small-
    group, 84–85
Intrinsic value *versus* stock value,
    98–99, 167–169, 171, 173–174
Investment bankers, 173–174
Investor Relations Department, 168
Investors, 149; legitimate concerns
    of, 169–171; listening to, sources
    of, 167–169; short-term *versus*
    long-term, 167–169, 171; social
    networks of, 172; strategy and,
    117; third-party influences on,
    171–172; working with, 167–172
ITV, 170

J

James F. Reda & Associates, 95
Job rotation, 134
Johnson (Chair, PSS/World Med-
    ical), 121
Johnson & Johnson, 95
JP Morgan Chase, 82

K

King John, 8
Kmart, 76, 78–79
Kodak, 127, 169–170
Koppes, R., 8
Kraft, 129
Krebs, R., 82
Krol, J., 33–34, 125

L

Lafley, A. G., 76
Lateral job moves, 134
Lead director: board candidate
    interview by, 156; CEO perfor-
    mance review and, 87, 91; CEO
    relationship and, 35–36, 37;
    choosing, 34–35; disruptive di-
    rectors and, 46; facilitation role
    of, 32–34; intermediary role of,
    35–36, 37; site visits by, 58; as
    strategy immersion session facili-
    tator, 122; Twelve-Month Agenda
    setting with, 70

Leaders, below-CEO: boardroom presentations by, 80–81, 136–137; getting information about, 135–136; informal contact with, 50, 81, 136; in leadership gene pool, 24, 129–138; lower-level, 137–138; recruiting outsiders for, 133; in succession pool, getting to know, 79–82, 135–138

Leadership development, 129–130, 134, 138

Leadership gene pool, 24, 129–138; board overview of, 133–136; board sampling of, 136–138; change and keeping relevant, 130–133; diversity in, 132–133; importance of, 129–130; meetings about, 160; time allocation for, 69; as top board question, 65, 129. *See also* Succession pool

Legal responsibilities, board education in, 159

Legal risks, 145, 146

Legislative risk, 146

Lewis, K., 78

Lexmark, 127

Liberated boards: characteristics of, 6, 7–9; CEO selection in, 75–76; dangers of, 8–9, 14–15; education for, 158; focus on substantive issues in, 17, 30; group dynamics in, 16, 17, 18–19, 30, 33; information architecture in, 17, 21, 47–48, 51; Sarbanes-Oxley Act and, 7; self-evaluations of, 42–43; transition to, 7–9, 18–19

Liquidity: *versus* growth, 140–143; monitoring, 25, 140–143; risk and, 145

Logistics, meeting, 160–166

London Business School, 26

Long-tail businesses, 96, 103

Long-term capital projects, 64–65

Long-term obligations, 65–66. *See also* Debt

Lucent, 140

Luke, J., 122

M

Management: commentary by, in board briefing, 53–54; executive sessions and, 36, 37, 39–41; strategy blueprint from, 125–127; in strategy immersion sessions, 120–121; Top Ten Questions and, 67. *See also Chief executive officer* headings

Management letter, 49, 54–56

Market research firms, 52–53

Market share information, 52, 53, 143

Marketing expertise, on board, 152

Matrix structure, 131–132

McColl, H., 78

McDonald's, 71, 85

McNerney, J., 138

MeadWestvaco, 10, 35, 122

Mechanics, 16; observable variables and, 25–26

Media, 174, 183

Medtronic, 82

Meetings: agenda development for, 160–165; closure of, 31–32; informal, 166; length of, 160; logistics of, 160–166; sample checklist for, 161–165; strategy immersion, 119–124; time allocation in, 22, 61–62. *See also* Focus on substantive issues; Group dynamics; Strategy immersion sessions

Messier, J.-M., 94

Micronic Laser Systems AB, 19

Microsoft, 132, 170

Milestones: CEO performance, 101; strategy, 127–128

Miller Brewing, 117

Minow, N., 8

Monitoring, 139–147; areas of, 25, 139, 140; financial health, 25, 140–143; operating performance, 25, 139, 140, 143–144; risk, 25, 144–147; strategy, 127–128; as top board concern, 65–66, 139–140

Monks, B., 8

Motorola, 169

N

Nardelli, B., 82, 138

National Association of Corporate
    Directors (NACD), Director of
    the Year, 35

Nationsbank, 78

NCNB, 78

NCR, 19

NDC Health, Annual Report and
    strategy blueprint, 177–181

Nepotism, 26

New Economy, 6, 99

Nitpicking, 15, 67–68, 155

Nominating Committee, 46, 158

Norms, for group interaction,
    30–32

Nortel, 102

Northrop Grumman, 71

Nyberg, L., 19, 22

NYSE requirements, 42, 51

O

Observable variables, 25–26, 183–184

Off-balance-sheet financing, 65

Office Depot, 97

Oil companies, 142, 170

Operating performance monitoring,
    25, 139, 140, 143–144

Organic growth, 64–65, 152

Organizational structure, leadership
    competencies and, 131–132

Outside candidates: assessment of,
    83–86; recruiting, into lower
    leadership ranks, 133

Ovitz, M., 94, 110, 159

P

Palmisano, S., 76

Pay for performance, 94, 98, 101. *See
    also* CEO compensation

Peer comparisons, for CEO compen-
    sation, 101–102

Peer evaluation, 42, 44

Peer relationships, 18

Pension funding, 65

Performance information, in board
    briefing, 50, 51–52

Performance measures and indica-
    tors, 25; in board briefing, 51–52;
    board education in, 159; for CEO
    compensation, 63, 98–101, 106–
    110; of intrinsic value *versus* stock
    value, 98–99; long-term and
    short-term, 99–101; for monitor-
    ing operating performance,
    143–144; research on board
    behavior and, 185; strategy and,
    124, 127–128; as top board con-
    cern, 66

Performance objectives, CEO: com-
    pensation philosophy and, 95–98;
    evaluating performance to, 87,
    91, 106–110; matching, with cash
    and equity, 101–106; setting,
    98–101

PerkinElmer, 130

Pharmaceutical companies, 52,
    64–65

Phases of board evolution, 6–10; di-
    agnostic questionnaire on, 11–13;
    differences among, 15–22. *See
    also* Ceremonial boards; Liber-
    ated boards; Progressive boards

Philip Morris, 129

Pitney Bowes, 50, 137

Political risk, 146

Popular, Inc., 145

Positioning, business, 115

Power problems, 18–20

Power vacuum, 19

Premature decisions: on CEO selec-
    tion, 83; in executive sessions, 39

Prestige factor, 35

Prime Computer, 76

Priorities, 22, 61–71. *See also* Focus
    on substantive issues

Procter & Gamble, 76, 129

Progressive boards: best practices of,
    for adding value, 23–25; building
    blocks of, 15–22; characteristics
    of, 6, 9–10, 14–15; CEO compen-
    sation set by, 23–24, 63, 94–112;
    CEO selection by, 23, 62–63,
    75–93; composition of, 151–156;

examples of, 10; focus on substantive issues in, 15, 17, 61–71; group dynamics in, 15, 16–20, 29–46; influencers and, 173–174; information architecture in, 15, 20–22, 47–60, 175; investor relationships with, 167–172; leadership gene pool and, 24, 65, 129–138; monitoring functions of, 25, 65–66, 139–147; operations of, 151–166; other boards *versus*, 15–22; strategy work of, 24, 64–65, 113–128; succession process of, 23, 62–63; transition to, 9–10, 174–176

Promotion practices, 134

PSS/World Medical board of directors: as Progressive, 10; strategy immersion sessions of, 118–119, 121, 122

Public scrutiny: Ceremonial boards and, 7; of CEO compensation, 94, 106, 110; as risk, 146; trend toward, 5–6, 8. *See also* Investors

Q

Quaker Oats, 117

R

Rabbit holes, 46

Ratings agencies, 52–53

Recession, 5–6

Red flags: about chief executive officer, 92; raised by analysts, 53

Reda, J., 95, 102, 106

Reference checking: of board candidates, 155–156; of CEO candidates, 84, 85

Reforms, 8

Register of Corporations, 183

Regulatory change, 55, 132, 146, 158

Report formats: board briefing, 54; management letter, 55–56

Reports: board briefing, 48, 50–54; committee, 49, 59–60; employee survey, 49, 56–57; leadership gene pool overview, 133–136; management letter, 49, 54–56; strategy blueprint, 125–127. *See also* Information architecture

Research, board and governance: agenda for, 183–186; based on clinical observation of decision making, 184–185; on causal relationships, 26, 183–186; framework of practices based on, 186; limitations of observable variables in, 25–26, 183–184; sample size for, 186; sources for traditional, 183–184

Resource allocation: compensation philosophy and, 97; information on, in board briefing, 52; strategy and, 116

Retention, of high-performers, 134–135

Retirement benefits, 106

Retreats, for strategy immersion sessions, 119, 123–124, 175

Reward systems, 135

Risk: annual meetings about, 160; board education in, 159; business, 145; CEO compensation and, 96; committee on, 147; financial, 141–142, 144, 145; legal, 145; liquidity health and, 141–142, 145; monitoring, 25, 144–147; operating, 144–147; strategy and, 125; types of, 96, 144–146

Risk Committee, 147, 158

Rohm and Haas, 57–58

Rubber-stamping boards, 7. *See also* Ceremonial boards

Ruettgers, M., 33

Rules of engagement, 29, 30–32, 46, 175

Ryder Systems, 97–98

S

SABMiller, 117

Salary, base, 101–102. *See also* CEO compensation

Sandvik, 19

Santa Fe Pacific, 82

Sarbanes-Oxley Act, 51, 154, 155; governance changes post-, 3–5, 6, 7, 8, 158

SBC, 102

Scandals: investor concerns and, 170; public scrutiny and, 5; Sarbanes-Oxley Act and, 8

Scott, L., 91

Search firms, 75–76, 85, 174

Securities and Exchange Commission (SEC), 8, 154

Seidenberg, I., 55

Selection, chief executive officer. *See* CEO selection

Self-evaluation, 10, 30, 42–44; NYSE requirement for, 42; of Progressive *versus* other boards, 20, 42–44

Self-interest, 171–172, 173–174

Semiconductor manufacturers, 52, 64–65

September 11, 2001, 6

Severance pay, 110–111

Shareholders. *See* Investors

Sherwin-Williams, 129

Signing bonuses, 110–111

Site visits, 57–58, 138

Small-group dynamics, 121–122

Smith, D., 118–119, 121

Snap-On, 19

Social responsibility, investor concerns about, 170

South African Breweries, 117

S&P 500 companies: with founding families, 26; total shareholder return comparisons to, 98, 104

Standard & Poor's Compustat, 183

Stanley Works, 129

Stempel, R., 8

Stock options, 103–104

Stock value *versus* intrinsic value, 98–99, 167–169, 171, 173–174

Strategy: board education in, 158–159; board role in, 24,
113–128; board understanding of, 63–64, 114–115; building blocks of, 114–115, 125; compensation philosophy and, 97, 124; consensus on, 123–124; essence of, 115, 125; external environment and, 115, 116–119, 120; immersion sessions on, 119–124, 175; information architecture and, 124; investor concerns about, 169–170; leadership competencies and, 131; linkages of, to other board work, 118; money-making linkage with, 63–64, 116, 125; monitoring, 127–128; practices in, 114; shaping and testing, 116–119; time allocation for, 69; as top board question, 63–64

Strategy blueprint, 125–127; sample, 177–181

Strategy immersion sessions, 119–124, 175; breakout groups of, 122–123; consensus in, 123–124; facilitation of, 121–122

Substantive issues focus. *See* Focus on substantive issues

Succession: assessing candidates for, 83–86; emergency, 70–71, 85–86, 176; internal candidates for, getting to know, 79–82, 135–138; investor concerns about, 170. *See also* CEO selection

Succession plan and process: board education in, 158; leadership gene pool and, 24, 65, 129–138; need for, 70–71, 75–76, 176; as top board concern, 23, 62–63, 75–76. *See also* CEO selection

Succession pool: diversity in, 81–82, 132–133; getting to know, 79–82, 135–138. *See also* Leadership gene pool

Sun Microsystems, 92

Suppliers, Wal-Mart, 146

Surveys: employee, 49, 56–57; evaluation, 43

T

Technology education, for board members, 159

Technology maps, 52

Telecom company, 128

Ten Questions Every Director Should Ask, 61, 62–67; management-board communication about, 67

Termination, of chief executive officer, 92–93

Teslik, S., 8

THLee Putnam Ventures, 107

3M, 129, 138

Time frame: for CEO compensation, 96; for CEO performance results, 86; for strategy immersion sessions, 119

Time management, 22, 61–62, 67–71. *See also* Focus on substantive issues

Time Warner, 102, 117

Timken Company, 122

Topics, for executive sessions, 38–39. *See also* Focus on substantive issues

Total shareholder return, as performance objective, 98–100

Truck test, 85

Trust: between chief executive officer and board, 35, 36, 38, 41, 48; information architecture and, 48

TRW, 71

Twelve-Month Agenda, 62, 67–71, 124, 175

Tyco, 8, 125; CEO and Chair roles at, 35–36, 37

U

Unilever, 129

Unisys, 136

United Kingdom, 170; non-executive Chairs in, 156–157

Unwanted directors: dissenting directors *versus*, 45; managing, 30, 45–46; recruiting and, 155

Unwritten rules, 30

Urgent concerns, in agenda, 69–71

V

Value adding: best practices for, 23–25, 73; Ceremonial boards and, 8–9; monitoring as, 139–140; by Progressive boards, 9–10, 23–25

Vanguard Guard, 168

Verizon, 55, 102

Vindictive ex-directors, 46

Vivendi Universal, 51, 117–118, 140, 143

W

W. R. Grace, 130

Wal-Mart, 64, 76, 78, 117, 146; CEO-board relationship at, 91; hypothetical discount retailer's competition with, 99–100, 105–106; supplier pressures from, 146

Wang Computer, 76

Web sites, for information sharing, 55–56

Weinbach, L., 136

Weissman, B., 50, 137

Welch, J., 79, 80, 82

What-ifs: to ask CEO candidates, 81; of equity awards, 103

WorldCom, 8, 96

X

Xerox, 130